WITHDRAWN

KF   Sex
9325   30360100035783
.S485
2013

NORTH ARKANSAS COLLEGE LIBRARY
1515 Pioneer Drive
Harrison, AR 72601

D1160072

TEEN RIGHTS AND FREEDOMS

| Sex

TEEN RIGHTS AND FREEDOMS

I Sex

David Haugen and Susan Musser
Book Editors

GREENHAVEN PRESS
A part of Gale, Cengage Learning

NORTH ARKANSAS COLLEGE LIBRARY
1515 Pioneer Drive
Harrison, AR 72601

GALE
CENGAGE Learning·

Detroit • New York • San Francisco • New Haven, Conn • Waterville, Maine • London

KF
9325
.S485
2013

Elizabeth Des Chenes, *Director, Publishing Solutions*

© 2013 Greenhaven Press, a part of Gale, Cengage Learning

Gale and Greenhaven Press are registered trademarks used herein under license.

For more information, contact:
Greenhaven Press
27500 Drake Rd.
Farmington Hills, MI 48331-3535
Or you can visit our Internet site at gale.cengage.com.

ALL RIGHTS RESERVED
No part of this work covered by the copyright herein may be reproduced, transmitted, stored, or used in any form or by any means graphic, electronic, or mechanical, including but not limited to photocopying, recording, scanning, digitizing, taping, Web distribution, information networks, or information storage and retrieval systems, except as permitted under Section 107 or 108 of the 1976 United States Copyright Act, without the prior written permission of the publisher.

For product information and technology assistance, contact us at:

Gale Customer Support, 1-800-877-4253.
For permission to use material from this text or product, submit all requests online at www.cengage.com/permissions.

Further permissions questions can be emailed to permissionrequest@cengage.com.

Articles in Greenhaven Press anthologies are often edited for length to meet page requirements. In addition, original titles of these works are changed to clearly present the main thesis and to explicitly indicate the author's opinion. Every effort is made to ensure the Greenhaven Press accurately reflects the original intent of the authors. Every effort has been made to trace the owners of copyrighted material.

Cover Image: © kovtynfoto/Shutterstock.com.

LIBRARY OF CONGRESS CATALOGING-IN-PUBLICATION DATA

Sex / David Haugen and Susan Musser, book editors.
pages cm. -- (Teen rights and freedoms)
Includes bibliographical references and index.
ISBN 978-0-7377-6404-8 (hardcover)
1. Sex and law--United States. 2. Teenagers--Legal status, laws, etc.--United States. 3. Teenagers--Sexual behavior--Government policy--United States. I. Haugen, David M., 1969- editor of compilation. II. Musser, Susan, editor of compilation.
KF9325.S485 2013
342.7308--dc23

2012046274

Printed in the United States of America
1 2 3 4 5 6 7 17 16 15 14 13

Contents

1. **A State Cannot Require Parental Consent for a Minor's Abortion**   11
   The US Supreme Court's Decision

   Harry Blackmun

   The US Supreme Court rules in 1976 that a Missouri law requiring parental consent for any minor's abortion violates a young woman's right to obtain an abortion as defined in the 1973 landmark Supreme Court case *Roe v. Wade.*

2. **States Should Have the Right to Require Parental Consent Before a Minor's Abortion**   17
   Concurring and Dissenting Opinion

   John Paul Stevens

   A US Supreme Court justice concurs with the decision in *Planned Parenthood of Central Missouri v. Danforth* (1976), but he defends the state's interest in protecting minors through the requiring of parental consent before an abortion.

3. **Parental Consent Can Be Required Before a Minor's Abortion Can Be Performed**   23
   The US Supreme Court's Decision

   Lewis F. Powell Jr.

The US Supreme Court finds in 1979 that laws requiring parental consent for a minor's abortion are constitutional as long as they provide an alternative path for the minor to obtain approval for the procedure.

unconstitutional because they limit young people's right to privacy and their right to protect their health.

A US Supreme Court justice maintains in 1981 that gender-neutral laws could be just as effective as gender-specific laws at deterring sex between a male and a minor female.

A writer contends that sexting is part of a young person's natural curiosity about sex and should not be dealt with as a criminal matter.

Foreword

*"In the truest sense freedom cannot be
bestowed, it must be achieved."*
                    Franklin D. Roosevelt,
                    September 16, 1936

The notion of children and teens having rights is a relatively recent development. Early in American history, the head of the household—nearly always the father—exercised complete control over the children in the family. Children were legally considered to be the property of their parents. Over time, this view changed, as society began to acknowledge that children have rights independent of their parents, and that the law should protect young people from exploitation. By the early twentieth century, more and more social reformers focused on the welfare of children, and over the ensuing decades advocates worked to protect them from harm in the workplace, to secure public education for all, and to guarantee fair treatment for youths in the criminal justice system. Throughout the twentieth century, rights for children and teens—and restrictions on those rights—were established by Congress and reinforced by the courts. Today's courts are still defining and clarifying the rights and freedoms of young people, sometimes expanding those rights and sometimes limiting them. Some teen rights are outside the scope of public law and remain in the realm of the family, while still others are determined by school policies.

Each volume in the Teen Rights and Freedoms series focuses on a different right or freedom and offers an anthology of key essays and articles on that right or freedom and the responsibilities that come with it. Material within each volume is drawn from a diverse selection of primary and secondary sources— journals, magazines, newspapers, nonfiction books, organization newsletters, position papers, speeches, and government documents, with a particular emphasis on Supreme Court and lower court decisions. Volumes also include first-person narratives from young people and others involved in teen rights issues, such as parents and educators. The material is selected and arranged to highlight all the major social and legal controversies relating to the right or freedom under discussion. Each selection is preceded by an introduction that provides context and background. In many cases, the essays point to the difference between adult and teen rights, and why this difference exists.

Many of the volumes cover rights guaranteed under the Bill of Rights and how these rights are interpreted and protected in regard to children and teens, including freedom of speech, freedom of the press, due process, and religious rights. The scope of the series also encompasses rights or freedoms, whether real or perceived, relating to the school environment, such as electronic devices, dress, Internet policies, and privacy. Some volumes focus on the home environment, including topics such as parental control and sexuality.

Numerous features are included in each volume of Teen Rights and Freedoms:

- An annotated **table of contents** provides a brief summary of each essay in the volume and highlights court decisions and personal narratives.
- An **introduction** specific to the volume topic gives context for the right or freedom and its impact on daily life.
- A brief **chronology** offers important dates associated with the right or freedom, including landmark court cases.
- **Primary sources**—including personal narratives and court decisions—are among the varied selections in the anthology.
- **Illustrations**—including photographs, charts, graphs, tables, statistics, and maps—are closely tied to the text and chosen to help readers understand key points or concepts.

- An annotated list of **organizations to contact** presents sources of additional information on the topic.
- A **for further reading** section offers a bibliography of books, periodical articles, and Internet sources for further research.
- A comprehensive subject **index** provides access to key people, places, events, and subjects cited in the text.

Each volume of Teen Rights and Freedoms delves deeply into the issues most relevant to the lives of teens: their own rights, freedoms, and responsibilities. With the help of this series, students and other readers can explore from many angles the evolution and current expression of rights both historic and contemporary.

Introduction

The sexuality of young people has always been a controversial topic in the United States. For many people, sexual relationships should entail a level of maturity that cannot be acquired in youth. Indeed, there is a pervasive notion that sex can end childhood by tainting it with supposedly adult knowledge. It is still common, for example, to hear the end of virginity referred to as a "loss of innocence." However, the preservation of that innocence is only one narrative in current discussions about teenage sexuality. While some adults mourn what they see as the early maturity of children today, others show concern that an unrealistic faith in childhood innocence might leave young people unaware of the rights and protections they need to negotiate the complexities of sexual initiation.

In a January 25, 1981, article for the *New York Times*, Mary Winn, the author of *Children Without Childhood*, describes how social changes since the 1960s pitted the idyllic concept of childhood against the media, modern psychiatry, and new attitudes toward sexual and individual freedom. Winn states that these factors made children more knowledgeable about sex and other adult issues and more cognizant of these issues in movies, television, literature, and magazines. According to Winn, adults aided this dismantling of childhood by loosening control over access to adult subject matter. Of modern children, Winn writes, "Their roles have changed from innocent, dependent, 'special' creatures, to secret and not-so-secret sharers of adult life's inevitable burdens." Current estimates of sexual activity among youth may seem to support the argument that promiscuity, for instance, abounds in recent years. The Guttmacher Institute reports in a 2012 fact sheet that seven of ten teens have had intercourse by age nineteen, with the average being age seventeen. Thirteen percent of teens reported having sex before age fifteen. The institute contends that the proportion of teens reporting having sex has remained fairly constant since 2002.

Despite the statistical facts verifying that kids are having sex, not everyone is panicked by such reports. In a December 5, 2011, *Salon* article citing new evidence that "sexting" (the sending of lewd images—usually of oneself—over a cell phone or the Internet) is not very prevalent among teenagers, Tracy Clark-Flory points out that adults still don't know whether American kids are "horny little devils or precious little angels." Clark-Flory suggests that national opinion seems to fluctuate "between the extreme poles of corruption and innocence" precisely because long-held stereotypes, targeted polls, common sense, and media scares continue to battle it out in adult perceptions of youth. Indeed, adults are never sure whether to be worried that their children are engaging in sexual activity, accepting that such behavior is normal, or content that today's youth are prepared and smart enough to make the right decisions when it comes to sex.

Amid this public outcry and debate, young people are navigating their path toward adulthood with mixed messages. Influences on teen sexual behavior come from many sources beyond the often-inconsistent counsel of adults that Clark-Flory mentions, and frequently the impressions these sources impart are incomplete or unbalanced. In a December 27, 2007, article for the *Boston Globe*, head of the Planned Parenthood League of Massachusetts Dianne Luby states, "A study by the Kaiser Family Foundation found that 70 percent of television shows include sexual content; yet at the same time, only 14 percent mention contraception, abstinence, or the consequences of sex." Making the right decisions about sex depends on an individual's understanding of the consequences of sexual activity and the rights each person possesses in relation to this activity.

Court rulings and laws have defined the parameters of sexual activity for minors, leaving young people at the mercy of adult decision-making. The overriding concern has always been to protect those who are deemed too impressionable and immature from making poor choices or from manipulation by others who are wise enough to know better. However, it is the young people who must live with both the consequences of their sexual behavior and the outcomes of public policy that seek to control it. That policy depends quite a bit on prevailing attitudes toward childhood and assumptions about the ability of young people to make appropriate choices about their own behavior and health. *Teen Rights and Freedoms: Sex* examines the rights young people have when facing major issues involving sex, such as age of consent, contraception access, and teen pregnancy.

Chronology

June 7, 1965	The US Supreme Court rules in *Griswold v. Connecticut* that it is unconstitutional for states to institute laws outlawing the use of contraceptives, finding these laws a violation of the right to marital privacy.
March 22, 1972	In *Eisenstadt v. Baird*, the US Supreme Court finds a Massachusetts law making it illegal for unmarried people to obtain contraceptive devices to be unconstitutional under the right to equal protection.
January 22, 1973	In *Roe v. Wade*, the US Supreme Court finds that the right to privacy, contained in the due process clause of the Fourteenth Amendment, protects a woman's right to have an abortion.
July 1, 1976	In *Planned Parenthood of Central Missouri v. Danforth*, the US Supreme Court upholds a woman's right to have an abortion, deeming the parental consent for minors requirement in Missouri state regulations unconstitutional.
June 9, 1977	The US Supreme Court rules in *Carey v. Population Services International* that it is unconstitutional to prohibit drugstores and pharmacies from selling

contraceptives to minors or advertising and displaying contraceptives.

October 31, 1977

In *Meloon v. Helgemoe*, the US First Circuit Court of Appeals in New Hampshire finds it unconstitutional for a state law to make it a felony for a male to have sexual intercourse with a female under the age of fifteen but lack any provisions making it a felony for female offenders.

July 2, 1979

The US Supreme Court rules in *Bellotti v. Baird* that states may require parental consent for a minor's abortion as long as the minor has an alternative means of obtaining permission for the procedure.

March 23, 1981

The US Supreme Court finds in *Michael M. v. Superior Court of Sonoma County* that laws punishing only males for statutory rape are not in violation of the Equal Protection Clause because young women face a higher risk from sexual intercourse, in the form of teen pregnancy, than young men.

June 15, 1983

The US Supreme Court rules in *Planned Parenthood Association of Kansas City, MO v. Ashcroft* that a provision in a Missouri law requiring minors to obtain consent for an abortion from parents or the juvenile court is constitutional.

June 25, 1990	In *Hodgson v. Minnesota*, the US Supreme Court finds that a Minnesota law requiring consent from both parents for a minor to have an abortion violates the US Constitution and puts pregnant teenagers at risk.
June 29, 1992	In *Planned Parenthood of Southeastern Pennsylvania v. Casey*, the US Supreme Court finds that parental consent may be required under state law before an abortion can be performed on a minor.
June 26, 2003	In *Lawrence v. Texas*, the US Supreme Court finds a Texas law that defines consensual homosexual intercourse between two adults as illegal sodomy to be in violation of the Fourteenth Amendment's protection of privacy. This ruling invalidates the sodomy laws still on the books in thirteen other states as well.
October 21, 2005	The Kansas Supreme Court rules in *State v. Limon* that it is unconstitutional to punish teens more severely for engaging in homosexual acts with other teens than teens who engage in heterosexual acts with other teens.
October 26, 2007	The Georgia Supreme Court finds in *Wilson v. State of Georgia* that the ten-year sentence handed down to Genarlow Wilson, who was convicted of aggravated child molestation in 2005

for engaging in oral sex with a fifteen year old when he was seventeen, was disproportionate.

October 2, 2009   The State Supreme Court of Iowa finds in *State of Iowa v. Bruegger* that the defendant's sentence of twenty-five years in prison for statutory rape constitutes cruel and unusual punishment, and he must be given a new sentencing hearing.

June 8, 2011   The Ohio Supreme Court rules in *In re D.B.* that in circumstances where two minors age thirteen or younger participate in a sexual act, neither can be convicted of statutory rape.

> *"Constitutional rights do not mature and come into being magically only when one attains the state-defined age of majority."*

A State Cannot Require Parental Consent for a Minor's Abortion

The US Supreme Court's Decision

Harry Blackmun

Soon after the US Supreme Court case Roe v. Wade *(1973) granted women the right to terminate unwanted pregnancies, Planned Parenthood and a pair of physicians challenged a Missouri law that required pregnant minors to attain parental consent before obtaining an abortion. In the following viewpoint, a US Supreme Court justice maintains that the state statute was unconstitutional. The court found that minors are endowed with the same rights afforded adults under the US Constitution and therefore can avail themselves of those rights affirmed by* Roe v. Wade. *Harry Blackmun served as an associate justice in the US Supreme Court from 1970 to 1994.*

Harry Blackmun, Court opinion, *Planned Parenthood of Central Missouri v. Danforth*, US Supreme Court, July 1, 1976.

Section 3(4) [of the Missouri bill] requires, with respect to the first 12 weeks of pregnancy, where the woman is unmarried and under the age of 18 years, the written consent of a parent or person *in loco parentis* [acting in place of a parent] unless, again, "the abortion is certified by a licensed physician as necessary in order to preserve the life of the mother." It is to be observed that only one parent need consent.

Two Conflicting Views

The appellees defend the statute in several ways. They point out that the law properly may subject minors to more stringent limitations than are permissible with respect to adults, and they cite, among other cases, *Prince v. Massachusetts* (1944), and *McKeiver v. Pennsylvania* (1971). Missouri law, it is said, "is replete with provisions reflecting the interest of the state in assuring the welfare of minors," citing statutes relating to a guardian *ad litem* [on behalf of another] for a court proceeding, to the care of delinquent and neglected children, to child labor, and to compulsory education. Certain decisions are considered by the State to be outside the scope of a minor's ability to act in his own best interest or in the interest of the public, citing statutes proscribing the sale of firearms and deadly weapons to minors without parental consent, and other statutes relating to minors' exposure to certain types of literature, the purchase by pawnbrokers of property from minors, and the sale of cigarettes and alcoholic beverages to minors. It is pointed out that the record contains testimony to the effect that children of tender years (even ages 10 and 11) have sought abortions. Thus, a State's permitting a child to obtain an abortion without the counsel of an adult "who has responsibility or concern for the child would constitute an irresponsible abdication of the State's duty to protect the welfare of minors."

Parental discretion, too, has been protected from unwarranted or unreasonable interference from the State, citing *Meyer v. Nebraska* (1923); *Pierce v. Society of Sisters* (1925); *Wisconsin v.*

Yoder (1972). Finally, it is said that § 3(4) imposes no additional burden on the physician, because, even prior to the passage of the Act, the physician would require parental consent before performing an abortion on a minor.

The appellants, in their turn, emphasize that no other Missouri statute specifically requires the additional consent of a minor's parent for medical or surgical treatment, and that, in Missouri, a minor legally may consent to medical services for pregnancy (excluding abortion), venereal disease, and drug abuse. The result of § 3(4), it is said, "is the ultimate supremacy of the parents' desires over those of the minor child, the pregnant patient." It is noted that, in Missouri, a woman under the age of

A St. Louis, Missouri, Planned Parenthood office advertises its services. In 1976, the US Supreme Court ruled in favor of Planned Parenthood of Missouri, stating that minors do not need to seek consent from parents before obtaining an abortion. © AP Images/James A. Finley.

18 who marries with parental consent does not require parental consent to abort, and yet her contemporary who has chosen not to marry must obtain parental approval.

The District Court majority recognized that, in contrast to § 3(3), the State's interest in protecting the mutuality of a marriage relationship is not present with respect to § 3(4). It found "a compelling basis," however, in the State's interest "in safeguarding the authority of the family relationship." The dissenting judge observed that one could not seriously argue that a minor must submit to an abortion if her parents insist, and he could not see "why she would not be entitled to the same right of self-determination now explicitly accorded to adult women, provided she is sufficiently mature to understand the procedure and to make an intelligent assessment of her circumstances with the advice of her physician."

Minors Are Protected by the US Constitution

Of course, much of what has been said [previously in the case], with respect to § 3(3) applies with equal force to § 3(4). Other courts that have considered the parental consent issue in the light of *Roe* [*v. Wade* (1973)] and *Doe* [*v. Bolton* (1973)] have concluded that a statute like § 3(4) does not withstand constitutional scrutiny.

We agree with appellants and with the courts whose decisions have just been cited that the State may not impose a blanket provision, such as § 3(4), requiring the consent of a parent or person *in loco parentis* as a condition for abortion of an unmarried minor during the first 12 weeks of her pregnancy. Just as with the requirement of consent from the spouse, so here, the State does not have the constitutional authority to give a third party an absolute, and possibly arbitrary, veto over the decision of the physician and his patient to terminate the patient's pregnancy, regardless of the reason for withholding the consent.

Constitutional rights do not mature and come into being magically only when one attains the state-defined age of majority.

PARENTAL CONSENT REQUIREMENTS FOR ABORTION BY STATE

PC   Parental consent
PN   Parental notification
NONE   No PC or PN are required now
2   Both parents required

State	Status	State	Status
Alabama	PC	Missouri	PC
Alaska	PN	Montana	NONE
Arizona	PC	Nebraska	PC
Arkansas	PC	Nevada	NONE
California	NONE	New Hampshire	PN
Colorado	PN	New Jersey	NONE
Connecticut	NONE	New Mexico	NONE
Delaware	PN	New York	NONE
District of		North Carolina	PC
Columbia	NONE	North Dakota	PC2
Florida	PN	Ohio	PC
Georgia	PN	Oklahoma	PN & PC
Hawaii	NONE	Oregon	NONE
Idaho	PC	Pennsylvania	PC
Illinois	NONE	Rhode Island	PC
Indiana	PC	South Carolina	PC
Iowa	PN	South Dakota	PN
Kansas	PC2	Tennessee	PC
Kentucky	PC	Texas	PN & PC
Louisiana	PC	Utah	PN & PC
Maine	NONE	Vermont	NONE
Maryland	PN	Virginia	PC
Massachusetts	PC	Washington	NONE
Michigan	PC	West Virginia	PN
Minnesota	PN2	Wisconsin	PC
Mississippi	PC2	Wyoming	PN & PC

Taken From: Coalition for Positive Sexuality, "Parental Consent," February 2012. www.positive.org.

Minors, as well as adults, are protected by the Constitution, and possess constitutional rights. The Court indeed, however, long has recognized that the State has somewhat broader authority to regulate the activities of children than of adults.

Prince v. Massachusetts [1944]; *Ginsberg v. New York* (1968). It remains, then, to examine whether there is any significant state interest in conditioning an abortion on the consent of a parent or person *in loco parentis* that is not present in the case of an adult.

One suggested interest is the safeguarding of the family unit and of parental authority. It is difficult, however, to conclude that providing a parent with absolute power to overrule a determination, made by the physician and his minor patient, to terminate the patient's pregnancy will serve to strengthen the family unit. Neither is it likely that such veto power will enhance parental authority or control where the minor and the nonconsenting parent are so fundamentally in conflict and the very existence of the pregnancy already has fractured the family structure. Any independent interest the parent may have in the termination of the minor daughter's pregnancy is no more weighty than the right of privacy of the competent minor mature enough to have become pregnant.

We emphasize that our holding that § 3(4) is invalid does not suggest that every minor, regardless of age or maturity, may give effective consent for termination of her pregnancy. The fault with § 3(4) is that it imposes a special consent provision, exercisable by a person other than the woman and her physician, as a prerequisite to a minor's termination of her pregnancy, and does so without a sufficient justification for the restriction. It violates the strictures of *Roe* and *Doe*.

| "*The State's interest in protecting a young person from harm justifies the imposition of restraints on his or her freedom.*"

States Should Have the Right to Require Parental Consent Before a Minor's Abortion

Concurring and Dissenting Opinion

John Paul Stevens

In the 1976 case Planned Parenthood of Central Missouri v. Danforth, *the US Supreme Court ruled that a Missouri statute impeded a pregnant minor's right to obtain an abortion by requiring parental consent for the procedure. In the following viewpoint, a US Supreme Court justice finds no evidence that the state's parental consent law is unconstitutional. According to the author, the states have a duty to ensure the well-being of minors and have enacted other laws that limit young people's rights. John Paul Stevens served as an associate justice of the US Supreme Court from 1975 to 2010.*

In *Roe v. Wade* [1973], the Court held that a woman's right to decide whether to abort a pregnancy is entitled to constitutional

John Paul Stevens, Concurring and dissenting opinion, *Planned Parenthood of Central Missouri v. Danforth*, US Supreme Court, July 1, 1976.

protection. That decision, which is now part of our law, answers the question discussed in Part IV-E of the Court's opinion, but merely poses the question decided in Part IV-D.

If two abortion procedures had been equally accessible to Missouri women, in my judgment, the United States Constitution would not prevent the state legislature from outlawing the one it found to be less safe even though its conclusion might not reflect a unanimous consensus of informed medical opinion. However, the record indicates that, when the Missouri statute was enacted, a prohibition of the saline amniocentesis procedure[1] was almost tantamount to a prohibition of any abortion in the State after the first 12 weeks of pregnancy. Such a prohibition is inconsistent with the essential holding of *Roe v. Wade*, and therefore cannot stand.

The State Has an Interest in the Welfare of Youth

In my opinion, however, the parental consent requirement is consistent with the holding in *Roe*. The State's interest in the welfare of its young citizens justifies a variety of protective measures. Because he may not foresee the consequences of his decision, a minor may not make an enforceable bargain. He may not lawfully work or travel where he pleases, or even attend exhibitions of constitutionally protected adult motion pictures. Persons below a certain age may not marry without parental consent. Indeed, such consent is essential even when the young woman is already pregnant. The State's interest in protecting a young person from harm justifies the imposition of restraints on his or her freedom even though comparable restraints on adults would be constitutionally impermissible. Therefore, the holding in *Roe v. Wade* that the abortion decision is entitled to constitutional protection merely emphasizes the importance of the decision; it does not lead to the conclusion that the state legislature has no power to enact legislation for the purpose of protecting a young pregnant woman from the consequences of an incorrect decision.

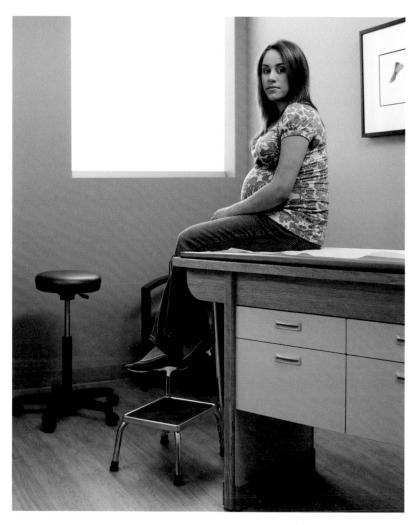

A teen waits in a doctor's office. US Supreme Court Justice John Paul Stevens argued that the state should have the power to protect a young pregnant woman from the consequences of an improper decision. © Thomas Barwick/Getty Images.

The abortion decision is, of course, more important than the decision to attend or to avoid an adult motion picture, or the decision to work long hours in a factory. It is not necessarily any more important than the decision to run away from home or the decision to marry. But even if it is the most important kind of a decision a young person may ever make, that assumption merely enhances the quality of the State's interest in maximizing the probability that the decision be made correctly, and with full understanding of the consequences of either alternative.

The Court recognizes that the State may insist that the decision not be made without the benefit of medical advice. But since the most significant consequences of the decision are not medical in character, it would seem to me that the State may, with equal legitimacy, insist that the decision be made only after other appropriate counsel has been had as well. Whatever choice a pregnant young woman makes—to marry, to abort, to bear her child out of wedlock—the consequences of her decision may have a profound impact on her entire future life. A legislative determination that such a choice will be made more wisely in most cases if the advice and moral support of a parent play a part in the decision-making process is surely not irrational. Moreover, it is perfectly clear that the parental consent requirement will necessarily involve a parent in the decisional process.

Parental Consent Ensures Pregnant Minors Make the Wisest Choice

If there is no parental consent requirement, many minors will submit to the abortion procedure without ever informing their parents. An assumption that the parental reaction will be hostile, disparaging, or violent no doubt persuades many children simply to bypass parental counsel which would, in fact, be loving, supportive, and, indeed, for some indispensable. It is unrealistic, in my judgment, to assume that every parent-child relationship is either (a) so perfect that communication and accord will take place routinely or (b) so imperfect that the absence of communication reflects the child's correct prediction that the parent will exercise his or her veto arbitrarily to further a selfish interest, rather than the child's interest. A state legislature may conclude that most parents will be primarily interested in the welfare of their children, and further, that the imposition of a parental consent requirement is an appropriate method of giving the parents an opportunity to foster that welfare by helping a pregnant distressed child to make and to implement a correct decision.

The State's interest is not dependent on an estimate of the impact the parental consent requirement may have on the total number of abortions that may take place. I assume that parents will sometimes prevent abortions which might better be performed; other parents may advise abortions that should not be performed. Similarly, even doctors are not omniscient; specialists in performing abortions may incorrectly conclude that the immediate advantages of the procedure outweigh the disadvantages which a parent could evaluate in better perspective. In each

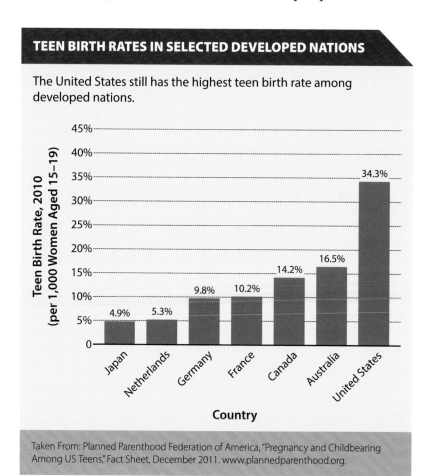

TEEN BIRTH RATES IN SELECTED DEVELOPED NATIONS

The United States still has the highest teen birth rate among developed nations.

Taken From: Planned Parenthood Federation of America, "Pregnancy and Childbearing Among US Teens," Fact Sheet, December 2011. www.plannedparenthood.org.

individual case, factors much more profound than a mere medical judgment may weigh heavily in the scales. The overriding consideration is that the right to make the choice be exercised as wisely as possible.

The Court assumes that parental consent is an appropriate requirement if the minor is not capable of understanding the procedure and of appreciating its consequences and those of available alternatives. This assumption is, of course, correct and consistent with the predicate which underlies all state legislation seeking to protect minors from the consequences of decisions they are not yet prepared to make. In all such situations, chronological age has been the basis for imposition of a restraint on the minor's freedom of choice even though it is perfectly obvious that such a yardstick is imprecise, and perhaps even unjust in particular cases. The Court seems to assume that the capacity to conceive a child and the judgment of the physician are the only constitutionally permissible yardsticks for determining whether a young woman can independently make the abortion decision. I doubt the accuracy of the Court's empirical judgment. Even if it were correct, however, as a matter of constitutional law I think a State has power to conclude otherwise, and to select a chronological age as its standard.

In short, the State's interest in the welfare of its young citizens is sufficient, in my judgment, to support the parental consent requirement.

Note

1. A saline amniocentesis is an obsolete technique in which a salt solution is injected into the uterus to induce abortion.

> *"We are not persuaded that, as a general rule, the requirement of obtaining both parents' consent unconstitutionally burdens a minor's right to seek an abortion."*

Parental Consent Can Be Required Before a Minor's Abortion Can Be Performed

The US Supreme Court's Decision

Lewis F. Powell Jr.

In Bellotti v. Baird *(1979), the US Supreme Court ruled that a Massachusetts law requiring minors to obtain parental consent for an abortion was unconstitutional because the state failed to offer alternative measures. In the following viewpoint, a US Supreme Court justice maintains that there is nothing to prevent states from requiring parental consent as long as minors can seek abortion through an alternative route such as the order of a judge. Lewis F. Powell Jr. served as an associate justice of the US Supreme Court from 1972 to 1987.*

A child, merely on account of his minority, is not beyond the protection of the Constitution. As the Court said in *In re*

Lewis F. Powell Jr., Majority opinion, *Bellotti v. Baird*, US Supreme Court, July 2, 1979.

Gault (1967), "whatever may be their precise impact, neither the Fourteenth Amendment nor the Bill of Rights is for adults alone." This observation, of course, is but the beginning of the analysis. The Court long has recognized that the status of minors under the law is unique in many respects. As Mr. Justice [Felix] Frankfurter aptly put it: "Children have a very special place in life which law should reflect. Legal theories and their phrasing in other cases readily lead to fallacious reasoning if uncritically transferred to determination of a State's duty towards children." *May v. Anderson* (1953). The unique role in our society of the family, the institution by which "we inculcate and pass down many of our most cherished values, moral and cultural," *Moore v. East Cleveland* (1977), requires that constitutional principles be applied with sensitivity and flexibility to the special needs of parents and children. We have recognized three reasons justifying the conclusion that the constitutional rights of children cannot be equated with those of adults: the peculiar vulnerability of children; their inability to make critical decisions in an informed, mature manner; and the importance of the parental role in child rearing.

The Unique Status of Children in Legal Matters

The Court's concern for the vulnerability of children is demonstrated in its decisions dealing with minors' claims to constitutional protection against deprivations of liberty or property interests by the State. With respect to many of these claims, we have concluded that the child's right is virtually coextensive with that of an adult. For example, the Court has held that the Fourteenth Amendment's guarantee against the deprivation of liberty without due process of law is applicable to children in juvenile delinquency proceedings. *In re Gault.* In particular, minors involved in such proceedings are entitled to adequate notice, the assistance of counsel, and the opportunity to confront their accusers. They can be found guilty only upon proof beyond a reasonable doubt, and they may assert the privilege against compulsory self-incrimination. *In re Winship* (1970). . . .

[Such] rulings have not been made on the uncritical assumption that the constitutional rights of children are indistinguishable from those of adults. Indeed, our acceptance of juvenile courts distinct from the adult criminal justice system assumes that juvenile offenders constitutionally may be treated differently from adults. In order to preserve this separate avenue for dealing with minors, the Court has said that hearings in juvenile delinquency cases need not necessarily "'conform with all of the requirements of a criminal trial or even of the usual administrative hearing.'" *In re Gault.* Thus, juveniles are not constitutionally entitled to trial by jury in delinquency adjudications. *McKeiver v. Pennsylvania* [1971]. Viewed together, our cases show that although children generally are protected by the same constitutional guarantees against governmental deprivations as are adults, the State is entitled to adjust its legal system to account for children's vulnerability and their needs for "concern, . . . sympathy, and . . . paternal attention." [*McKeiver v. Pennsylvania.*]

Second, the Court has held that the States validly may limit the freedom of children to choose for themselves in the making of important, affirmative choices with potentially serious consequences. These rulings have been grounded in the recognition that, during the formative years of childhood and adolescence, minors often lack the experience, perspective, and judgment to recognize and avoid choices that could be detrimental to them.

Ginsberg v. New York (1968), illustrates well the Court's concern over the inability of children to make mature choices, as the First Amendment rights involved are clear examples of constitutionally protected freedoms of choice. At issue was a criminal conviction for selling sexually oriented magazines to a minor under the age of 17 in violation of a New York state law. It was conceded that the conviction could not have stood under the First Amendment if based upon a sale of the same material to an adult. Notwithstanding the importance the Court always has attached to First Amendment rights, it concluded that "even where there is an invasion of protected freedoms 'the power of the state to control the conduct of children reaches beyond the scope of its authority over adults. . . .'" The Court was convinced that the New York Legislature rationally could conclude that the sale to children of the magazines in question presented a danger against which they should be guarded. It therefore rejected the argument that the New York law violated the constitutional rights of minors.

The Role of Parental Consent

Third, the guiding role of parents in the upbringing of their children justifies limitations on the freedoms of minors. The State commonly protects its youth from adverse governmental action and from their own immaturity by requiring parental consent to or involvement in important decisions by minors. But an additional and more important justification for state deference to parental control over children is that "[t]he child is not the mere creature of the State; those who nurture him and direct his destiny have the right, coupled with the high duty, to recognize and prepare him for additional obligations." *Pierce v. Society of Sisters* (1925). "The duty to prepare the child for 'additional obligations' . . . must be read to include the inculcation of moral standards, religious beliefs, and elements of good citizenship." *Wisconsin v. Yoder* (1972). This affirmative process of teaching, guiding, and inspiring by precept and example is essential to the growth of young people into mature, socially responsible citizens.

We have believed in this country that this process, in large part, is beyond the competence of impersonal political institutions. Indeed, affirmative sponsorship of particular ethical, religious, or political beliefs is something we expect the State not to attempt in a society constitutionally committed to the ideal of individual liberty and freedom of choice. Thus, "[i]t is cardinal with us that the custody, care and nurture of the child reside first in the parents, whose primary function and freedom include

Judge Lewis F. Powell stands in front of the US Supreme Court building. He wrote the majority opinion that decided that states may require parental consent for abortion so long as there is an alternative means of consent. © AP Images/Stuart T. Wagner.

preparation for obligations the state can neither supply nor hinder." *Prince v. Massachusetts* [1944].

Unquestionably, there are many competing theories about the most effective way for parents to fulfill their central role in assisting their children on the way to responsible adulthood. While we do not pretend any special wisdom on this subject, we cannot ignore that central to many of these theories, and deeply rooted in our Nation's history and tradition, is the belief that the parental role implies a substantial measure of authority over one's children. Indeed, "constitutional interpretation has consistently recognized that the parents' claim to authority in their own household to direct the rearing of their children is basic in the structure of our society." *Ginsberg v. New York*.

Properly understood, then, the tradition of parental authority is not inconsistent with our tradition of individual liberty; rather, the former is one of the basic presuppositions of the latter. Legal restrictions on minors, especially those supportive of the parental role, may be important to the child's chances for the full growth and maturity that make eventual participation in a free society meaningful and rewarding. Under the Constitution, the State can "properly conclude that parents and others, teachers for example, who have [the] primary responsibility for children's well-being are entitled to the support of laws designed to aid discharge of that responsibility." *Ginsberg v. New York*.

Do Parental Consent Requirements Violate the US Constitution?

With these principles in mind, we consider the specific constitutional questions presented by these appeals. In 12S, Massachusetts has attempted to reconcile the constitutional right of a woman, in consultation with her physician, to choose to terminate her pregnancy as established by *Roe v. Wade* (1973), and *Doe v. Bolton* (1973), with the special interest of the State in encouraging an unmarried pregnant minor to seek the advice of her parents in making the important decision whether or not to bear a child. . . . We previously had held in *Planned Parenthood of Central Missouri v. Danforth* (1976), that a State could not lawfully authorize an absolute parental veto over the decision of a minor to terminate her pregnancy. [In *Bellotti v. Baird* (1976)], we recognized that [Massachusetts statute] 12S could be read as "fundamentally different from a statute that creates a 'parental veto,'" thus "avoid[ing] or substantially modify[ing] the federal constitutional challenge to the statute." The question before us—in light of what we have said in the prior cases—is whether 12S, as authoritatively interpreted by the Supreme Judicial Court, provides for parental notice and consent in a manner that does not unduly burden the right to seek an abortion.

Appellees and intervenors contend that even as interpreted by the Supreme Judicial Court of Massachusetts 12S does unduly burden this right. They suggest, for example, that the mere requirement of parental notice constitutes such a burden. As stated . . . above, however, parental notice and consent are qualifications that typically may be imposed by the State on a minor's right to make important decisions. As immature minors often lack the ability to make fully informed choices that take account of both immediate and long-range consequences, a State reasonably may determine that parental consultation often is desirable and in the best interest of the minor. It may further determine, as a general proposition, that such consultation is particularly desirable with respect to the abortion decision—one that for some people raises profound moral and religious concerns. As Mr. Justice [Potter] Stewart wrote in concurrence in *Planned Parenthood of Central Missouri v. Danforth*:

> There can be little doubt that the State furthers a constitutionally permissible end by encouraging an unmarried pregnant minor to seek the help and advice of her parents in making the very important decision whether or not to bear a child. That is a grave decision, and a girl of tender years, under emotional stress, may be ill-equipped to make it without mature advice

and emotional support. It seems unlikely that she will obtain adequate counsel and support from the attending physician at an abortion clinic, where abortions for pregnant minors frequently take place.

But we are concerned here with a constitutional right to seek an abortion. The abortion decision differs in important ways from other decisions that may be made during minority. The need to preserve the constitutional right and the unique nature of the abortion decision, especially when made by a minor, require a State to act with particular sensitivity when it legislates to foster parental involvement in this matter.

States Must Provide Pregnant Teens Alternative Measures to Obtain an Abortion

The pregnant minor's options are much different from those facing a minor in other situations, such as deciding whether to marry. A minor not permitted to marry before the age of majority is required simply to postpone her decision. She and her intended spouse may preserve the opportunity for later marriage should they continue to desire it. A pregnant adolescent, however, cannot preserve for long the possibility of aborting, which effectively expires in a matter of weeks from the onset of pregnancy.

Moreover, the potentially severe detriment facing a pregnant woman is not mitigated by her minority. Indeed, considering her probable education, employment skills, financial resources, and emotional maturity, unwanted motherhood may be exceptionally burdensome for a minor. In addition, the fact of having a child brings with it adult legal responsibility, for parenthood, like attainment of the age of majority, is one of the traditional criteria for the termination of the legal disabilities of minority. In sum, there are few situations in which denying a minor the right to make an important decision will have consequences so grave and indelible.

Yet, an abortion may not be the best choice for the minor. The circumstances in which this issue arises will vary widely. In a given case, alternatives to abortion, such as marriage to the father of the child, arranging for its adoption, or assuming the responsibilities of motherhood with the assured support of family, may be feasible and relevant to the minor's best interests. Nonetheless, the abortion decision is one that simply cannot be postponed, or it will be made by default with far-reaching consequences.

For these reasons, as we held in *Planned Parenthood of Central Missouri v. Danforth*, "the State may not impose a blanket provision . . . requiring the consent of a parent or person in loco parentis [acting in place of the parent] as a condition for abortion of an unmarried minor during the first 12 weeks of her pregnancy." Although, as stated [above], such deference to parents may be permissible with respect to other choices facing a minor, the unique nature and consequences of the abortion decision make it inappropriate "to give a third party an absolute, and possibly arbitrary, veto over the decision of the physician and his patient to terminate the patient's pregnancy, regardless of the reason for withholding the consent." We therefore conclude that if the State decides to require a pregnant minor to obtain one or both parents' consent to an abortion, it also must provide an alternative procedure whereby authorization for the abortion can be obtained.

A pregnant minor is entitled in such a proceeding to show either: (1) that she is mature enough and well enough informed to make her abortion decision, in consultation with her physician, independently of her parents' wishes; or (2) that even if she is not able to make this decision independently, the desired abortion would be in her best interests. The proceeding in which this showing is made must assure that a resolution of the issue, and any appeals that may follow, will be completed with anonymity and sufficient expedition to provide an effective opportunity for an abortion to be obtained. In sum, the procedure must ensure that the provision requiring parental consent does not in fact amount to the "absolute, and possibly arbitrary, veto" that was found impermissible in *Danforth.*

Aspects of the Massachusetts Law Are Unconstitutional

It is against these requirements that 12S must be tested. We observe initially that as authoritatively construed by the highest court of the State, the statute satisfies some of the concerns that require special treatment of a minor's abortion decision. It provides that if parental consent is refused, authorization may be "obtained by order of a judge of the superior court for good cause shown, after such hearing as he deems necessary." A superior court judge presiding over a 12S proceeding "must disregard all parental objections, and other considerations, which are not based exclusively on what would serve the minor's best interests." The Supreme Judicial Court also stated: "Prompt resolution of a [12S] proceeding may be expected. . . . The proceeding need not be brought in the minor's name and steps may be taken, by impoundment or otherwise, to preserve confidentiality as to the minor and her parents. . . . [W]e believe that an early hearing and decision on appeal from a judgment of a Superior Court judge may also be achieved." The court added that if these expectations were not met, either the superior court, in the exercise of its rule-making power, or the Supreme Judicial Court would be willing to eliminate any undue burdens by rule or order.

Despite these safeguards, which avoid much of what was objectionable in the statute successfully challenged in *Danforth,* 12S falls short of constitutional standards in certain respects. We now consider these.

Among the questions certified to the Supreme Judicial Court was whether 12S permits any minors—mature or immature—to obtain judicial consent to an abortion without any parental consultation whatsoever. The state court answered that, in general, it does not. "[T]he consent required by [12S must] be obtained for every nonemergency abortion where the mother is less than eighteen years of age and unmarried." The text of 12S itself states an exception to this rule, making consent unnecessary from any parent who has "died or has deserted his or her family." The Supreme Judicial Court construed the statute as containing an additional exception: Consent need not be obtained "where no parent (or statutory substitute) is available." The court also ruled that an available parent must be given notice of any judicial proceedings brought by a minor to obtain consent for an abortion.

We think that, construed in this manner, 12S would impose an undue burden upon the exercise by minors of the right to seek an abortion. As the District Court recognized, "there are parents who would obstruct, and perhaps altogether prevent, the minor's right to go to court" [*Baird v. Bellotti* (1978)]. There is no reason to believe that this would be so in the majority of cases where consent is withheld. But many parents hold strong views on the subject of abortion, and young pregnant minors, especially those living at home, are particularly vulnerable to their parents' efforts to obstruct both an abortion and their access to court. It would be unrealistic, therefore, to assume that the mere existence of a legal right to seek relief in superior court provides an effective avenue of relief for some of those who need it the most.

We conclude, therefore, that under state regulation such as that undertaken by Massachusetts, every minor must have the opportunity—if she so desires—to go directly to a court without first consulting or notifying her parents. If she satisfies the court that she is mature and well enough informed to make intelligently the abortion decision on her own, the court must authorize her to act without parental consultation or consent. If she fails to satisfy the court that she is competent to make this decision independently, she must be permitted to show that an abortion nevertheless would be in her best interests. If the court is persuaded that it is, the court must authorize the abortion. If, however, the court is not persuaded by the minor that she is mature or that the abortion would be in her best interests, it may decline to sanction the operation.

There is, however, an important state interest in encouraging a family rather than a judicial resolution of a minor's abortion decision. Also, as we have observed above, parents naturally take an interest in the welfare of their children—an interest that is particularly strong where a normal family relationship exists and where the child is living with one or both parents. These factors properly may be taken into account by a court called upon to determine whether an abortion in fact is in a minor's best interests. If, all things considered, the court determines that an abortion is in the minor's best interests, she is entitled to court authorization without any parental involvement. On the other hand, the court may deny the abortion request of an immature minor in the absence of parental consultation if it concludes that her best interests would be served thereby, or the court may in such a case defer decision until there is parental consultation in which the court may participate. But this is the full extent to which parental involvement may be required. For the reasons stated above, the constitutional right to seek an abortion may not be unduly burdened by state-imposed conditions upon initial access to court.

Parents Have an Interest in Determining a Child's Best Course of Action

Section 12S requires that both parents consent to a minor's abortion. The District Court found it to be "custom" to perform other medical and surgical procedures on minors with the consent of only one parent, and it concluded that "nothing about abortions . . . requires the minor's interest to be treated differently" [*Baird v. Bellotti* (1975)].

We are not persuaded that, as a general rule, the requirement of obtaining both parents' consent unconstitutionally burdens a minor's right to seek an abortion. The abortion decision has implications far broader than those associated with most other kinds of medical treatment. At least when the parents are together and the pregnant minor is living at home, both the father and mother have an interest—one normally supportive—in helping to determine the course that is in the best interests of a daughter. Consent and involvement by parents in important decisions by minors long have been recognized as protective of their immaturity. In the case of the abortion decision, for reasons we have stated, the focus of the parents' inquiry should be the best interests of their daughter. As every pregnant minor is entitled in the first instance to go directly to the court for a judicial determination without prior parental notice, consultation, or consent, the general rule with respect to parental consent does not unduly burden the constitutional right. Moreover, where the pregnant minor goes to her parents and consent is denied, she still must have recourse to a prompt judicial determination of her maturity or best interests.

The Role of a Judge in a Teen's Ability to Obtain an Abortion

Another of the questions certified by the District Court to the Supreme Judicial Court was the following: "If the superior court finds that the minor is capable [of making], and has, in fact, made and adhered to, an informed and reasonable decision to have an abortion, may the court refuse its consent based on a finding that a parent's, or its own, contrary decision is a better one?" To this the state court answered:

> [W]e do not view the judge's role as limited to a determination that the minor is capable of making, and has made, an informed and reasonable decision to have an abortion. Certainly the judge must make a determination of those circumstances, but, if the statutory role of the judge to determine the best interests of the minor is to be carried out, he must make a finding on the basis of all relevant views presented to him. We suspect that the judge will give great weight to the minor's determination, if informed and reasonable, but in circumstances where he determines that the best interests of the minor will not be served by an abortion, the judge's determination should

prevail, assuming that his conclusion is supported by the evidence and adequate findings of fact.

The Supreme Judicial Court's statement reflects the general rule that a State may require a minor to wait until the age of majority before being permitted to exercise legal rights independently. But we are concerned here with the exercise of a constitutional right of unique character. As stated above, if the minor satisfies a court that she has attained sufficient maturity to make a fully informed decision, she then is entitled to make her abortion decision independently. We therefore agree with the District Court that 12S cannot constitutionally permit judicial disregard of the abortion decision of a minor who has been determined to be mature and fully competent to assess the implications of the choice she has made.

The Massachusetts Statute Falls Short

Although it satisfies constitutional standards in large part, 12S falls short of them in two respects: First, it permits judicial authorization for an abortion to be withheld from a minor who is found by the superior court to be mature and fully competent to make this decision independently. Second, it requires parental consultation or notification in every instance, without affording the pregnant minor an opportunity to receive an independent judicial determination that she is mature enough to consent or that an abortion would be in her best interests. Accordingly, we affirm the judgment of the District Court insofar as it invalidates this statute and enjoins its enforcement.

| "For young women who happen to be in
the wrong court at the wrong time . . .
they may spend a lifetime paying for
that bad luck."

No Choice for Teens

Amy Bach

*In the following viewpoint, a US Court of Appeals clerk argues that
parental consent laws regarding minors seeking abortion are unfair
and limit young people's rights. Although the US Supreme Court
found in* Planned Parenthood v. Casey *(1992) that states must
offer alternatives when mandating parental consent, the author believes this ruling has been ineffective for youth. She argues that this
bypass procedure has proven difficult or illusionary in states that
route these requests through pro-life judges. The author contends
that such politicking is a blatant disregard for a woman's right to
abortion as established by the landmark ruling in* Roe v. Wade
*(1973). Amy Bach is a clerk for the US Court of Appeals for the
Eleventh Circuit in Miami, Florida.*

In 1992, in *Planned Parenthood v. Casey*, the Supreme Court
ruled that a state may require a young woman who wants an
abortion to obtain her parents' consent—as long as there is a "bypass procedure" that allows her to apply for consent from a judge

Amy Bach, "No Choice for Teens," *The Nation*, vol. 269, no. 11, October 11, 1999, pp. 6–7.
Copyright © The Nation. All rights reserved. Reproduced by permission.

instead. At the time, abortion rights advocates bemoaned the *Casey* decision for severely narrowing the scope of *Roe v. Wade*, but few could have imagined just how paper-thin young women's right to choose might soon become.

In many of the forty-two states that now have parental notification laws (including New Jersey, signed into law by "prochoice" Governor Christine Todd Whitman), antiabortion judges have been highly creative when faced with pregnant minors who want their consent for abortions: using harassing interrogation tactics, appointing antichoice attorneys to represent the young women, and even—in a few cases whose implications are still unfolding—assigning lawyers to represent the interests of fetuses.

Juvenile Judge Mark Anderson in Montgomery, Alabama, has made no secret of his antiabortion proclivities, explaining in written decisions his "fixed opinion that abortion is wrong" and routinely denying parental consent waivers because the young

A teen girl reacts to a pregnancy test. Many argue that increased parental consent laws limit a woman's right to obtain an abortion. © beyond/Corbis.

women hadn't proved their "maturity" (the standard mandated by *Casey*). He is quite clear that demonstrating maturity in his courtroom means accepting his view of abortion. In denying consent to a 16-year-old, he wrote, "She goes to church but she testified that she had not considered the spiritual aspects of her decision." Judge Anderson also found that although she did receive counseling from a reproductive health clinic on the medical risks of abortion and assistance available to unwed mothers, she had not "sought counseling from a group or facility which opposes abortion . . . would it not be more convincing evidence of her maturity if she had . . . on her own . . . gone to hear the other side?"

It was in another case, involving a 17-year-old, that Judge Anderson decided to appoint a lawyer to represent the fetus. The judge explained that he wanted to give the "unborn child" a "guardian ad litem" (an agent of the court usually appointed to represent children's interests) to assure that the fetus had "an opportunity to have a voice, even a vicarious one, in the decision making."

The young woman's own court-appointed lawyer had carefully prepped her client, a high school honors student who had a scholarship for college. She told the court that she believed abortion was a sin, that if any complications arose she realized that it would be God's punishment and that she had sought counseling with a group called Sav-A-Life, where she had cradled a rubber fetus doll in her hands. She explained that she could not ask her mother for consent because her mother had told her that if she ever got pregnant she could not live at home and would receive no help. She also feared violence from her father, who had been known to point a gun at boys who looked at her provocatively.

Enter the fetus's guardian, Montgomery attorney Julian McPhillips, who had given his "client" a name, "Baby Ashley." Over numerous constitutional objections by the young woman's counsel, according to transcripts of the closed hearing, McPhillips proceeded methodically. "You say that you are aware that God instructed you not to kill your own baby, but you want to do it anyway? And are you saying here today that notwith-standing everything that you want to interfere with God's plan for your baby?"

"I think that is between me and God," she said.

McPhillips continued. "And you are not concerned after you have had the abortion that someday you may wake up and say my gosh, what have I done to my own baby?"

"It may happen," she said.

"You are not worried about being haunted by this? Here you have the chance to save the life of your own baby. . . . And still you want to go ahead and snuff out the life of your own baby?"

"Yes."

After four hours of what Judge Anderson called "argument of the most acrimonious nature," he made the "regretful" finding that the girl was indeed well informed. The Alabama Court of Appeals denied an appeal from McPhillips on Baby Ashley's be-half, on the basis that only the young woman could appeal. The girl obtained the abortion, but she still regards her experience with Judge Anderson as a horrible ordeal. "He's a son of a bitch," she told her lawyer.

When the local press heard about Judge Anderson's new guardian-ad-litem [on behalf of another] policy, it ran news sto-ries and uncomplimentary editorials, and judicial higher-ups stopped assigning parental consent cases to him. But his tactics won him a following among antiabortion activists, and Alabama legislators soon proposed a law permitting a judge to appoint a guardian ad litem for the fetus of every underage woman seeking an abortion, "so that the court may make an informed decision and do substantial justice." With Attorney General Bill Pryor's support, the Alabama House passed the bill earlier this year [1999]. It didn't make it to the Senate, but it will be reintroduced in the next session early next year.

Pro-choice advocates across the country can rattle off the names of juvenile judges they advise girls to avoid in almost every county. Judge James Payne in Indianapolis, for example,

US PUBLIC OPINION ON SPECIFIC ABORTION RESTRICTIONS

Do you favor or oppose each of the following proposals?

	Favor	Oppose
A law requiring doctors to inform patients about certain possible risks of abortion before performing the procedure	87%	11%
A law requiring women under 18 to get parental consent for any abortion	71%	27%
A law requiring women seeking abortions to wait 24 hours before having the procedure done	69%	28%
A law requiring women seeking an abortion to be shown an ultrasound image of her fetus at least 24 hours before the procedure	50%	46%
A law allowing pharmacists and health providers to opt out of providing medicine or surgical procedures that result in abortion	46%	51%

Taken From: Lydia Saad, "Common State Abortion Restrictions Spark Mixed Reviews," Gallup Politics, July 25, 2011. www.gallup.com.

routinely appointed antiabortion lawyers to represent pregnant girls. Others in Mississippi and Alabama require visits to an anti-abortion counseling center before granting a hearing. And in Arkansas, Alabama and Ohio, minors have to travel miles to get to a judge who may actually grant a bypass.

The appeals process offers some relief. When a Florida judge appointed a guardian ad litem for a fetus, the state's highest court overturned his decision. An Indianapolis juvenile judge was similarly overruled. Yet other than the appellate courts, there are few checks on judges operating in closed hearings. Meanwhile, Congress is deliberating a backdoor means of reinforcing "fetal rights" with the Unborn Victims of Violence Act, a bill that would make injuring a fetus—or even a fertilized egg—while committing a federal crime into a new criminal offense. The law would have the effect of defining fetuses at all stages of development as persons, which could potentially jeopardize abortion rights.

The actions of Judge Anderson and others show how far we have fallen since *Roe*, whose central tenet was that before viability, a woman's right to choose always trumps the rights of the fetus. For young women who happen to be in the wrong court at the wrong time, the balance has shifted in the opposite direction, and they may spend a lifetime paying for that bad luck.

> "It is precisely . . . when a teen's life or health is threatened by a pregnancy, that parental involvement is most needed and most helpful."

Parental Consent Laws Protect the Health of Minors

Teresa S. Collett

In the following viewpoint, a law professor argues that the US Congress needs to pass interstate parental notification laws to guard against minors crossing state lines to seek abortions. The author claims that parental notification is important both to the health of the young women involved and to make sure that the fathers— who are often older men—are made accountable for any applicable rape charges. She maintains that most Americans favor parental consent laws, and very few ill effects are reported in instances when parents are notified despite their child's wishes. Teresa S. Collett is a professor of law at the University of St. Thomas School of Law in Minneapolis, Minnesota.

On March 8, [2012] the U.S. House of Representatives Subcommittee on the Constitution heard testimony on the proposed Child Interstate Abortion Notification Act (CIANA). I

Teresa S. Collett, "Parental Consent Protects Young Women's Health," *Public Discourse*, March 29, 2012. www.thepublicdiscourse.com Copyright © 2012 by the Witherspoon Institute. All rights reserved. Reproduced by permission.

was among those who testified in favor of the Act. CIANA would prohibit transporting a minor across state lines with the intent that she obtain an abortion without involving her parents as may be required by her home state. It also would require that abortion providers comply with the parental notification or consent laws of a minor's home state when performing an abortion on a non-resident minor. More controversially, CIANA would require 24 hours' notice to the girl's parents if she was not a resident in the state where the abortion is being performed. All of these requirements would be waived in the event of a medical emergency threatening the girl's life or if the girl certified that she was the victim of parental abuse.

Consent Laws Are Favored by a Majority of Americans

The *New York Times* criticized the Act in an editorial titled "Yet Another Curb on Abortion." The editors called CIANA "mean-spirited," "constitutionally suspect," and "callous." It is none of these things. It is, in fact, a popular commonsense proposal that is fully constitutional.

There is a national consensus in favor of parental involvement laws, notwithstanding the controversial nature of abortion laws more generally. For more than three decades, polls have consistently reflected that over 70 percent of Americans support parental consent laws. Most recently a Gallup poll released July 25, 2011, showed that 71 percent of Americans support a law requiring parental consent prior to performance of an abortion on a minor. According to a 2009 Pew Research poll "Even among those who say abortion should be legal in most or all cases, 71% favor requiring parental consent."

Forty-five states have passed laws requiring parental notice or consent, although only thirty-seven states' laws are in effect at the moment due to constitutional challenges by abortion rights activists. And the weakest of these laws allow notice to or consent by other adult relatives of girls seeking abortion.

Various reasons underlie the popular support of these laws. As Justices [Sandra Day] O'Connor, [Anthony] Kennedy, and [David] Souter observed in *Planned Parenthood v. Casey* [1992], parental involvement laws for abortions "are based on the quite reasonable assumption that minors will benefit from consultation with their parents and that children will often not realize that their parents have their best interests at heart."

Parental Involvement Laws Have Very Few Negative Effects

The *New York Times* editorial disputed this claim, criticizing CIANA on the basis that teens "have reason to fear a violent reaction" and will "resort to unsafe alternatives."

These objections are repeatedly voiced by abortion activists. Yet they ignore published studies, many of them by the Guttmacher Institute, a research institute founded by Planned Parenthood, demonstrating that less than half of pregnant teens

A pregnant teen talks with her mother. A large portion of Americans believe that a pregnant teenager would benefit from consultation with her parents about a pregnancy. © Thinkstock Images/Getty Images.

tell their parents of their pregnancy and very few experience ill effects from the disclosure.

According to a national study conducted by researchers associated with Guttmacher, disappointment is the most common response of parents who learn that their teen daughter is pregnant, and almost no parent responds with violence. Teens reported an increase in parental stress as the most common consequence of disclosing their pregnancy. Less than half of one percent of the teens reported that they were "beaten."

The claim that minors will resort to unsafe alternatives is equally bogus. A 2007 study of self-induced medical abortions reported no cases involving children or adolescents. Similarly, notwithstanding the fact that parental involvement laws have been on the books in various states for over thirty years, there has been no case in which it has been established that a minor was injured as the result of obtaining an illegal or self-induced abortion in an attempt to avoid parental involvement.

What has been established, however, is that many teen pregnancies are the result of coercion and statutory rape. National studies reveal that almost two thirds of adolescent mothers have partners older than twenty years of age. In a study of over 46,000 pregnancies by school-age girls in California, researchers found that 71 percent, or over 33,000, were fathered by adult post-high-school men who were an average of five years older than the mothers. Perhaps even more shocking was the finding that men aged twenty-five years or older father more births among California school-age girls than do boys under age eighteen. Parental involvement laws are just one way the law can attempt to protect young girls from the predatory practices of some men.

Consent Laws Fight Sexual Exploitation and Protect Children's Health

Mandatory reporting of statutory rape and other sex crimes is another. Yet as evidenced by recent news stories, some abortion providers refuse to comply with reporting laws. Instead of reporting underage sex to state authorities who can then investigate and protect a girl from future abuse, clinics intentionally remain ignorant of the circumstances giving rise to the pregnancy. Clinics in Kansas have even gone so far as to argue in federal court that twelve-year-old children have a right to keep their sexual activities private and thus reporting laws are unconstitutional. Thankfully this absurd claim was rejected, but only on appeal from a district court ruling embracing the clinics' argument.

In addition to providing some protection against sexual exploitation of minors, the Supreme Court has identified three ways in which teens may benefit medically from parental involvement. First, parents are more likely to have greater experience in selecting medical providers and thus be able "to distinguish the competent and ethical from those that are incompetent or unethical." This benefit should not be lightly ignored, as evidenced by the horrific practices engaged in by Kermit Gosnell in Philadelphia, an abortion provider currently being prosecuted for multiple murders in connection with his abortion practice.

Second, parents can provide additional information about the minor's medical history—information a minor may not know, remember, or be willing to share. This can be particularly important where there is a history of depression or other mental disorder that may impact the minor's post-abortion psychological health. While claims of "post-abortion trauma" are hotly disputed, no one questions that women with a history of depression may be more susceptible to post-abortion mental health problems.

Finally, parents who know their daughter has undergone an abortion can more readily identify any post-procedure problems such as infection or hemorrhaging—two of the most common post-abortion complications. If caught early, both infection and hemorrhaging can be dealt with easily, but if ignored, either can lead to other complications or even death.

Opponents of CIANA argue that the Act would endanger teen health, and they criticize the emergency exception to parental involvement, which is limited to the life of the minor. This objection, like the other objections, ignores reality and constitutional precedents. In the five years between 2005 and 2010, the Wisconsin Department of Health reported almost 3,200 abortions performed on minors. Not a single one involved a medical emergency. During the same five years in Alabama, where over 4,500 abortions were performed on minors, only two involved a medical emergency. In Nebraska, of the 13,596 abortions performed on all women from 2005 to 2010, only three involved a medical emergency.

Evidence shows that of all teens obtaining abortions, only a tiny fraction of one percent occur in emergency circumstances. In *Gonzales v. Carhart* [2007], the United States Supreme Court upheld the constitutionality of the federal partial-birth abortion ban that contained a similarly narrow emergency exception, in part because of evidence that no broader exception was necessary.

Independent of the fact that such emergencies are so rare, it is precisely in these circumstances, when a teen's life or health is threatened by a pregnancy, that parental involvement is most needed and most helpful.

Interstate Legislation Is Needed

It is beyond dispute that young girls are being taken to out-of-state clinics in order to procure secret abortions. Abortion clinic operators in states without parental involvement laws routinely advertise in neighboring states where clinics must obtain parental consent or provide parental notice. For example, abortion providers in Granite City, Illinois have advertised Illinois's absence of any parental involvement requirement to Missouri minors, which has a parental consent law, for decades.

Missouri legislators attempted to stop this practice by passing a law creating civil remedies for parents and their daughters against individuals who would "intentionally cause, aid, or assist a minor" in obtaining an abortion without parental consent

Consent Laws Safeguard Parental Rights

Parental involvement laws are necessary for the protection of parental rights. Parents have a right to know if their minor child will be undergoing an abortion, an invasive and often dangerous surgical procedure. The constitutional and traditional right of parents to rear their children has long been acknowledged by the courts. The USSC [US Supreme Court in *Ginsberg v. New York* (1968)] states that "constitutional interpretation has consistently recognized that the parents' claim to authority in their own household to direct the rearing of their children is basic in the structure of our society."

Maggie Datiles, "Parental Involvement Laws for Abortion: Protecting Both Minors and Their Parents," Americans United for Life, April 23, 2010. www.aul.org.

or a judicial bypass. Abortion providers immediately attacked the law as unconstitutional, but it was upheld by the Missouri Supreme Court. The Court limited its opinion, however, by the observation that "Missouri simply does not have the authority to make lawful out-of-state conduct actionable here, for its laws do not have extraterritorial effect."

The proposed Child Interstate Abortion Notification Act is an appropriate and measured response to the limitations on state powers in our federalist system. It is grounded by the reality that parents are nearly always the first to help a teen in trouble, and that fact does not change when the "trouble" is an unplanned pregnancy. There is no other elective surgery that minors can obtain while keeping their parents in the dark, and the controversy surrounding this Act shows just how severely the judicial creation of abortion rights has distorted American law.

*"We would rather have not known that
our daughter had had an abortion, if
it meant that she could have . . . come
back home safely to us."*

Parents Fault Parental Consent Laws for Their Daughter's Death After an Unsafe Abortion

Personal Narrative

Bill and Karen Bell

*In the following viewpoint, the parents of a teen who died due to
complications from an illegal abortion relate their daughter's experience. Bill and Karen Bell argue that their daughter, Becky, was
forced to obtain a "back alley" abortion for an unwanted pregnancy because Indiana's state laws forbade minors from seeking
such services without parental consent. Becky believed her parents
would have been disappointed to learn of the pregnancy, and she
sought the only help available. The Bells argue that consent laws
need to be overturned, or more families will face similar tragedies.*

Bill and Karen Bell, "Patient Stories: Parental Involvement: Feature Story," National Abortion Federation. www.prochoice.org. Copyright © the National Abortion Federation. All
rights reserved. Reproduced by permission.

Sixteen years ago we would have supported legislation mandating parental involvement laws. Bills have been introduced by legislators to require minors under the age of 18 to notify their parents before obtaining an abortion, and to require minors to receive their parent's consent for an abortion. While these pieces of legislation seem reasonable on the surface, our experience has taught us that parental involvement laws seriously endanger the very families and teens they are intended to protect.

Learning the Sad Truth

In 1988, our beautiful, vibrant, 17-year-old daughter Becky died suddenly, after a six-day illness. The pathologist who directed her autopsy concluded that the cause of her death was streptococcus pneumonia, brought about by an illegal abortion. Learning this, we finally understood our daughter's last words. In the hospital, she had taken off her oxygen mask and said, "Mom, Dad, I love you. Forgive me."

How could this have happened? Why would Becky have risked an illegal abortion? How could parents as close to their daughter as we had always been not have known that she was pregnant and desperate to deal with a situation that she believed she couldn't share with us?

We learned the sad answers to these questions in the weeks following our daughter's death. Becky had told her girlfriends that she believed we would be terribly hurt and disappointed in her if she told us about her pregnancy. Like a lot of young people, she was not comfortable sharing intimate details of her developing sexuality with her parents.

State Laws Have Fatal Consequences

Becky discovered that our state has a parental consent law, which requires girls under the age of 18 to get their parent's permission before they can get an abortion. A Planned Parenthood counselor told her that she could apply for a judicial bypass as an alternative to parental consent. The counselor remembered

Why Some Young People Do Not Consider the Judicial Bypass Option for Abortion Consent

The judicial bypass procedure is required to be speedy and to protect the young woman's privacy, but rarely achieves these goals in practice. In Ohio, the judicial bypass procedure can take up to 22 days, pushing many young women into riskier, more expensive, second trimester abortions. . . .

In some states, judicial bypass is a time-consuming, costly and humiliating experience with little or no benefit to the teen. Young women who have used the judicial bypass procedure report that it was more traumatic than the actual abortion procedure. The typical teen reports that she was embarrassed and humiliated to have to explain her sexual life to an unfamiliar authority figure. . . .

Significant numbers of young women do seek judicial bypass. Most of these teens, however, are from middle and upper class families. Minors who are poor, less educated, more wary of the court system or who live in rural areas are far less able or likely to seek a bypass. For those who do not live in counties where court hearings are held or who must consider absence from school or work, transportation and other expenses, judicial bypass may not be an option. In some counties, judges routinely deny all bypass applications, effectively eliminating this alternative.

Susan Flinn et al., "Adolescent Abortion and Mandated Parental Involvement: The Impact of Back Alley Laws on Young Women," Center for Population Options, 1993.

Becky's response: "If I can't talk to my parents, how can I tell a judge who doesn't even know me?" We now know that in over ten years on the bench, the judge in our district has never issued a waiver to a teen for an abortion.

Desperate to avoid telling us about her pregnancy, and therefore unable to go to a reputable medical establishment, where abortions are provided compassionately and safely every day, Becky found someone operating outside the law who would help her. Becky had a back alley abortion. Indiana's parental involvement law ultimately led our daughter to her death.

Studies have established that the majority of teenagers (60–70%) do talk to their parents when they become pregnant. Of those who don't, about one-third are at risk of physical or emotional abuse. The rest, like Becky, believe for myriad reasons that this is a problem they must face without their parents.

Parental involvement laws further isolate girls in this last category, who feel it is impossible to turn to their parents, forcing them to instead make decisions and arrangements on their own.

Laws Cannot Enforce Family Communication

All parents would want to know if their child was in a situation like Becky's. In fact, we would have supported the law in our state before we experienced the loss of our daughter. We have been forced to learn in the most painful way imaginable that laws cannot create family communication. We would rather have not known that our daughter had had an abortion, if it meant that she could have obtained the best of care, and come back home safely to us.

Many of you have daughters and granddaughters, and we are sure that you would want to be involved in any issues relating to their health and well-being—just as we did. Yet, the law in Indiana did not force Becky to involve us at her most desperate time.

As much as we would have wanted to help Becky through this crisis, the law did not succeed in forcing her to talk to us about issues she found too upsetting to share with us. For the sake of other parents' daughters, we urge legislators who are considering these very dangerous bills to remember Becky Bell, and to pass no laws that will increase the chances that even one desperate girl will feel that her only choice is an illegal abortion.

The law in Indiana did not make Becky come to us. Will other parental involvement laws be any different?

> *"Limiting the distribution of nonprescription contraceptives to licensed pharmacists clearly imposes a significant burden on the right of the individuals to use contraceptives if they choose to do so."*

Minors Have the Right to Access Contraceptives

The US Supreme Court's Decision

William J. Brennan

In the 1977 case Carey v. Population Services International, *the US Supreme Court ruled that a New York law forbidding the sale of contraception to individuals under the age of sixteen was unconstitutional. In the following viewpoint, a US Supreme Court justice argues that the law unjustly restricted young people and other individuals from safeguarding their sexual health. Furthermore, he argues that the court supports the right of privacy in regards to choices of contraception and pregnancy. William J. Brennan served as an associate justice of the US Supreme Court from 1956 to 1990.*

Although "[t]he Constitution does not explicitly mention any right of privacy," the Court has recognized that one

William J. Brennan, Majority opinion, *Carey v. Population Services International*, US Supreme Court, June 9, 1977.

aspect of the "liberty" protected by the Due Process Clause of the Fourteenth Amendment is "a right of personal privacy, or a guarantee of certain areas or zones of privacy." *Roe v. Wade* (1973). This right of personal privacy includes "the interest in independence in making certain kinds of important decisions." *Whalen v. Roe* (1977). While the outer limits of this aspect of privacy have not been marked by the Court, it is clear [as the Court affirmed in *Roe v. Wade*] that among the decisions that an individual may make without unjustified government interference are personal decisions

> relating to marriage, *Loving v. Virginia* (1967); procreation, *Skinner v. Oklahoma ex rel. Williamson* (1942); contraception, *Eisenstadt v. Baird* [1972]; family relationships, *Prince v. Massachusetts* (1944); and childrearing and education, *Pierce v. Society of Sisters* (1925); *Meyer v. Nebraska* (1923).

The decision whether or not to beget or bear a child is at the very heart of this cluster of constitutionally protected choices. That decision holds a particularly important place in the history of the right of privacy, a right first explicitly recognized in an opinion holding unconstitutional a statute prohibiting the use of contraceptives, *Griswold v. Connecticut* [1965], and most prominently vindicated in recent years in the contexts of contraception, *Griswold v. Connecticut; Eisenstadt v. Baird*; and abortion, *Roe v. Wade, Doe v. Bolton* (1973); *Planned Parenthood of Central Missouri v. Danforth* (1976). This is understandable, for in a field that, by definition, concerns the most intimate of human activities and relationships, decisions whether to accomplish or to prevent conception are among the most private and sensitive. [In *Eisenstadt v. Baird*, the Court concluded]

> If the right of privacy means anything, it is the right of the individual, married or single, to be free of unwarranted governmental intrusion into matters so fundamentally affecting a person as the decision whether to bear or beget a child.

Assessing State Interest in Minors' Contraception Choices

That the constitutionally protected right of privacy extends to an individual's liberty to make choices regarding contraception does not, however, automatically invalidate every state regulation in this area. The business of manufacturing and selling contraceptives may be regulated in ways that do not infringe protected individual choices. And even a burdensome regulation may be validated by a sufficiently compelling state interest. In *Roe v. Wade*, for example, after determining that the "right of privacy . . . encompass[es] a woman's decision whether or not to terminate her pregnancy," we cautioned that the right is not absolute, and that certain state interests (in that case, "interests in safeguarding health, in maintaining medical standards, and in protecting potential life") may at some point "become sufficiently compelling to sustain regulation of the factors that govern the abortion decision." "Compelling" is of course the key word; where a decision as fundamental as that whether to bear or beget a child is involved, regulations imposing a burden on it may be justified only by compelling state interests, and must be narrowly drawn to express only those interests.

With these principles in mind, we turn to the question whether the District Court was correct in holding invalid the provisions of § 6811(8) as applied to the distribution of nonprescription contraceptives.

The US Constitution Protects an Individual's Right to Access Contraception

We consider first the wider restriction on access to contraceptives created by § 6811(8)'s prohibition of the distribution of nonmedical contraceptives to adults except through licensed pharmacists.

Appellants argue that this Court has not accorded a "right of access to contraceptives" the status of a fundamental aspect of personal liberty. They emphasize that *Griswold v. Connecticut* struck down a state prohibition of the use of contraceptives, and so had no occasion to discuss laws "regulating their manufacture or sale." *Eisenstadt v. Baird* was decided under the Equal Protection Clause, holding that "whatever the rights of the individual to access to contraceptives may be, the rights must be the same for the unmarried and the married alike." Thus appellants

In 1977 the US Supreme Court ruled that the state could not limit the sale of contraceptives, as it obstructs the right of a woman to protect herself against unwanted pregnancy or disease. © Charles Thatcher/Getty Images.

argue that neither case should be treated as reflecting upon the State's power to limit or prohibit distribution of contraceptives to any persons, married or unmarried.

The fatal fallacy in this argument is that it overlooks the underlying premise of those decisions that the Constitution protects

> the right of the individual . . . to be free from unwarranted governmental intrusion into . . . the decision whether to bear or beget a child.

Griswold did state that, by "forbidding the use of contraceptives, rather than regulating their manufacture or sale," the Connecticut statute there had "a maximum destructive impact" on privacy rights. This intrusion into "the sacred precincts of marital bedrooms" made that statute particularly "repulsive." But subsequent decisions have made clear that the constitutional protection of individual autonomy in matters of childbearing is not dependent on that element. *Eisenstadt v. Baird*, holding that the protection is not limited to married couples, characterized the protected right as the "*decision* whether to bear or beget a child." Similarly, *Roe v. Wade* held that the Constitution protects "a woman's *decision* whether or not to terminate her pregnancy." These decisions put *Griswold* in proper perspective. *Griswold* may no longer be read as holding only that a State may not prohibit a married couple's use of contraceptives. Read in light of its progeny, the teaching of *Griswold* is that the Constitution protects individual decisions in matters of childbearing from unjustified intrusion by the State.

Limiting Access Impinges on Personal Freedom

Restrictions on the distribution of contraceptives clearly burden the freedom to make such decisions. A total prohibition against sale of contraceptives, for example, would intrude upon individual decisions in matters of procreation and contraception as harshly as a direct ban on their use. Indeed, in practice, a prohibition against all sales, since more easily and less offensively enforced, might have an even more devastating effect upon the freedom to choose contraception. . . .

Limiting the distribution of nonprescription contraceptives to licensed pharmacists clearly imposes a significant burden on the right of the individuals to use contraceptives if they choose to do so. *Eisenstadt v. Baird.* The burden is, of course, not as great as that under a total ban on distribution. Nevertheless, the restriction of distribution channels to a small fraction of the total number of possible retail outlets renders contraceptive devices considerably less accessible to the public, reduces the opportunity for privacy of selection and purchase, and lessens the possibility of price competition. Of particular relevance here is *Doe v. Bolton*, in which the Court struck down, as unconstitutionally burdening the right of a woman to choose abortion, a statute requiring that abortions be performed only in accredited hospitals, in the absence of proof that the requirement was substantially related to the State's interest in protecting the patient's health. The same infirmity infuses the limitation in § 6811(8). [As the Court clarified in *Eisenstadt v. Baird*]

> Just as in *Griswold*, where the right of married persons to use contraceptives was "diluted or adversely affected" by permitting a conviction for giving advice as to its exercise . . . so here, to sanction a medical restriction upon distribution of a contraceptive not proved hazardous to health would impair the exercise of the constitutional right.

The State Has Not Proved Compelling Interest

There remains the inquiry whether the provision serves a compelling state interest. Clearly, [as *Roe v. Wade* states] "interests . . . in maintaining medical standards, and in protecting potential life," cannot be invoked to justify this statute. Insofar as § 6811(8) applies to nonhazardous contraceptives, it bears no relation to the State's interest in protecting health. *Eisenstadt v. Baird.* Nor is the interest in protecting potential life implicated in state regulation of contraceptives. *Roe v. Wade.*

Appellants therefore suggest that § 6811(8) furthers other state interests. But none of them is comparable to those the Court has heretofore recognized as compelling. Appellants argue that the limitation of retail sales of nonmedical contraceptives to pharmacists (1) expresses "a proper concern that young people not sell contraceptives"; (2) "allows purchasers to inquire as to the relative qualities of the varying products and prevents anyone from tampering with them"; and (3) facilitates enforcement of the other provisions of the statute. The first hardly can justify the statute's incursion into constitutionally protected rights, and, in any event, the statute is obviously not substantially related to any goal of preventing young people from selling contraceptives. Nor is the statute designed to serve as a quality control device. Nothing in the record suggests that pharmacists are particularly qualified to give advice on the merits of different nonmedical contraceptives, or that such advice is more necessary to the purchaser of contraceptive products than to consumers of other nonprescription items. Why pharmacists are better able or more inclined than other retailers to prevent tampering with prepackaged products, or, if they are, why contraceptives are singled out for this special protection, is also unexplained. As to ease of enforcement, the prospect of additional administrative inconvenience has not been thought to justify invasion of fundamental constitutional rights.

Regulating the Conduct of Minors

The District Court also held unconstitutional, as applied to nonprescription contraceptives, the provision of § 6811(8) prohibiting the distribution of contraceptives to those under 16 years of age. Appellants contend that this provision of the statute is constitutionally permissible as a regulation of the morality of minors, in furtherance of the State's policy against promiscuous sexual intercourse among the young.

The question of the extent of state power to regulate conduct of minors not constitutionally regulable when committed
by adults is a vexing one, perhaps not susceptible of precise answer. We have been reluctant to attempt to define "the totality of
the relationship of the juvenile and the state." *In re Gault* (1967).
Certain principles, however, have been recognized. "Minors, as
well as adults, are protected by the Constitution, and possess
constitutional rights." *Planned Parenthood of Central Missouri v.
Danforth.* "[W]hatever may be their precise impact, neither
the Fourteenth Amendment nor the Bill of Rights is for adults
alone." *In re Gault.* On the other hand, we have held in a variety
of contexts that "the power of the state to control the conduct of
children reaches beyond the scope of its authority over adults."
Prince v. Massachusetts (1944).

Of particular significance to the decision of this case, the
right to privacy in connection with decisions affecting procreation extends to minors, as well as to adults. *Planned Parenthood
of Central Missouri v. Danforth* held that a State

> may not impose a blanket provision . . . requiring the con-
> sent of a parent or person *in loco parentis* [acting in place of
> the parent] as a condition for abortion of an unmarried minor
> during the first 12 weeks of her pregnancy.

As in the case of the spousal consent requirement struck
down in the same case, "the State does not have the constitutional authority to give a third party an absolute, and possibly
arbitrary, veto," "'which the state itself is absolutely and totally
prohibited from exercising.'" State restrictions inhibiting privacy
rights of minors are valid only if they serve "any significant state
interest . . . that is not present in the case of an adult." *Planned
Parenthood* found that no such interest justified a state requirement of parental consent.

Since the State may not impose a blanket prohibition, or even
a blanket requirement of parental consent, on the choice of a minor to terminate her pregnancy, the constitutionality of a blanket

prohibition of the distribution of contraceptives to minors is *a fortiori* [with greater certainty] foreclosed. The State's interests in protection of the mental and physical health of the pregnant minor, and in protection of potential life are clearly more implicated by the abortion decision than by the decision to use a nonhazardous contraceptive.

Access to Contraception Does Not Lead to Increased Sexual Activity

Appellants argue, however, that significant state interests are served by restricting minors' access to contraceptives, because free availability to minors of contraceptives would lead to increased sexual activity among the young, in violation of the policy of New York to discourage such behavior. The argument is that minors' sexual activity may be deterred by increasing the hazards attendant on it. The same argument, however, would support a ban on abortions for minors, or indeed support a prohibition on abortions, or access to contraceptives, for the unmarried, whose sexual activity is also against the public policy of many States. Yet, in each of these areas, the Court has rejected the argument, noting in *Roe v. Wade* that "no court or commentator has taken the argument seriously." The reason for this unanimous rejection was stated in *Eisenstadt v. Baird:*

> It would be plainly unreasonable to assume that [the State] has prescribed pregnancy and the birth of an unwanted child [or the physical and psychological dangers of an abortion] as punishment for fornication.

We remain reluctant to attribute any such "scheme of values" to the State.

Moreover, there is substantial reason for doubt whether limiting access to contraceptives will, in fact, substantially discourage early sexual behavior. Appellants themselves conceded in the District Court that "there is no evidence that teenage extramarital sexual activity increases in proportion to the availability

A Judge Defends New York's Ability to Limit Teen Access to Contraception

No questions of religious belief, compelled allegiance to a secular creed, or decisions on the part of married couples as to procreation, are involved here. New York has simply decided that it wishes to discourage unmarried minors under 16 from having promiscuous sexual intercourse with one another. Even the Court would scarcely go so far as to say that this is not a subject with which the New York Legislature may properly concern itself. . . .

The majority of New York's citizens are in effect told that however deeply they may be concerned about the problem of promiscuous sex and intercourse among unmarried teenagers, they may not adopt this means of dealing with it. The Court holds that New York may not use its police power to legislate in the interests of its concept of the public morality as it pertains to minors. The Court's denial of a power so fundamental to self-government must, in the long run, prove to be but a temporary departure from a wise and heretofore settled course of adjudication to the contrary. I would reverse the judgment of the District Court.

William Rehnquist, Dissenting opinion,
Carey v. Population Services International,
US Supreme Court, June 9, 1977.

of contraceptives," and accordingly offered none, in the District Court or here. Appellees, on the other hand, cite a considerable body of evidence and opinion indicating that there is no such deterrent effect. Although we take judicial notice . . . that with or without access to contraceptives, the incidence of sexual activity among minors is high, and the consequence of such activity are frequently devastating, the studies cited by appellees play no part in our decision.

*"Requiring teens to tell a parent before
they can access contraceptive services
doesn't reduce their sexual activity—
it will just put their health and lives
at risk."*

Limiting Teens' Access to Contraception Unless They Obtain Parental Consent Puts Them at Risk

American Civil Liberties Union

*In the following viewpoint, a civil liberties organization argues
that the US Constitution and several key court cases endorse young
people's right to acquire contraception without parental consent.
The author contends that denying teens access to contraception
does not reduce sexual activity, but instead leads to more unwanted
pregnancies and the spread of sexually transmitted diseases. The
American Civil Liberties Union is a national organization dedicated to fighting for personal liberties and constitutional rights.*

Today, in every state, sexually active teenagers can get contraceptives to protect themselves against unplanned pregnancies and sexually transmitted diseases—even if they can't talk

American Civil Liberties Union, "Preventing Teenagers from Getting Contraceptives
Unless They Tell a Parent Puts Teens at Risk," July 18, 2003. www.aclu.org. Copyright
© 2003 by the American Civil Liberties Union. All rights reserved. Reproduced by
permission.

about sex with their parents. But some state and federal lawmakers want to take away teens' ability to protect themselves. They want to prevent sexually active teenagers from getting birth control unless they first tell their parents.

These proposals would radically alter long-standing public health policy and put teenagers at risk. Studies show that preventing teens from getting contraceptives unless they tell a parent won't stop teenagers from having sex. It will just drive them away from the services they need to protect themselves, leading to higher rates of unintended pregnancies and sexually transmitted diseases (STDs), including HIV. For these reasons, the leading medical organizations oppose laws that would require teens to involve their parents before they can get contraception. Such laws would endanger teens' health and lives and violate their rights.

Preventing Teenagers from Getting Contraception Doesn't Decrease Sexual Activity

Some people say that allowing teenagers to get contraceptives without first telling a parent encourages them to become sexually active and that, conversely, requiring teenagers to tell their parents before they get birth control would discourage sexual activity. But research about how teenagers behave flatly contradicts this theory. Teenagers don't become sexually active because they can go to a family planning provider and get contraceptives confidentially. In fact, on average, young women in the U.S. have been sexually active for 22 months before their first visit to a family planning provider. And studies show that making contraceptives available to teenagers does not increase sexual activity. Students in schools that make condoms available without requiring parental notification are *less* likely to have ever had sexual intercourse than students at schools that don't provide condoms confidentially. Moreover, in schools where condoms are readily available, those teens who do have sex are twice as likely as other students to have used a condom during their last sexual encounter.

The research thus shows that requiring teens to tell a parent before they can access contraceptive services doesn't reduce their sexual activity—it will just put their health and lives at risk. For example, a recent study published in the *Journal of the American Medical Association* looked at what sexually active teenage girls seeking services at family planning clinics in Wisconsin would do if they could not get prescription contraceptives unless the clinic notified their parents. The results are important for anyone who cares about teenagers' well-being:

- 47 percent of sexually active teenage girls said that they would stop accessing *all* reproductive health care services from the clinic if they couldn't get contraceptives without first telling their parents. Not only would these teenagers

RATES OF SEXUALLY TRANSMITTED DISEASES AMONG 15- TO 19-YEAR-OLDS IN THE UNITED STATES

STD	Cases	Rate per 100,000
Chlamydia	Males Females	730.46 3,314.69
Gonorrhea	Males Females	248.33 565.99
Primary and Secondary Syphilis	Males Females	5.98 3.28

Taken From: Centers for Disease Control and Prevention, Sexually Transmitted Diseases Interactive Data 2009, July 2012. www.cdc.org.

stop getting contraceptive services, they would also stop getting testing and treatment for STDs, including HIV;

- Another 12 percent would stop using some reproductive health care services or would delay testing or treatment for HIV or other STDs;
- This means that altogether 59 percent of sexually active teenage girls would stop or delay getting critical health care services; yet
- 99 percent of these teens—the ones who would stop or delay getting contraceptive services or STD testing and treatment—said they would continue having sex.

As this research shows, guarantees of confidentiality are one of the prime factors influencing whether a teenager will seek vital health services. In fact, in a nationwide study, the leading reason teenagers gave for not getting health care they knew they needed was concerns about confidentiality.

Limiting Teen Access to Contraception Puts Their Lives at Risk

Cutting off teenagers' access to contraceptives doesn't stop them from having sex, it just drives them out of doctors' offices. When teenagers don't visit family planning providers, not only do they forego contraceptive services, they also miss or dangerously postpone screening and treatment for STDs, routine gynecological exams, and other vital health care services. Teenagers are already a high risk population:

- Over half of all new HIV infections in the United States occur in adolescents.
- Every year three million U.S. teenagers contract a sexually transmitted disease. Left undetected and untreated, STDs can have lifelong consequences, including infertility.
- Teenage girls have the highest reported rates of chlamydia and gonorrhea.

• Close to 900,000 teenagers get pregnant each year. Four out of 10 girls get pregnant at least once before they turn 20.

If teenagers are prevented from getting contraceptives unless they involve a parent, these alarming numbers are likely to increase. A sexually active teen who does not use contraception has a 90 percent chance of getting pregnant within one year. In a single act of unprotected sex with an infected partner, a teenage girl has a 1 percent risk of acquiring HIV, a 30 percent risk of getting genital herpes, and a 50 percent chance of contracting gonorrhea.

Medical Groups Oppose Parental Consent Laws

Medical experts caution that when teenagers cannot obtain contraceptives without involving a parent, they are less likely to protect themselves from unintended pregnancy and STDs. For this reason, the leading medical organizations, including the American

A teenage couple selects contraceptives at a drug store. The ACLU argues that limiting access to contraceptives will not reduce teen sex and therefore puts teens at risk of pregnancy and sexually transmitted diseases. © Pauline St. Denis/Corbis.

Medical Association, the American Academy of Pediatrics, the American Academy of Family Physicians, the American College of Obstetricians and Gynecologists, the American Public Health Association, and the Society for Adolescent Medicine, among others, oppose laws that would require teens to involve a parent.

These groups have been vocal opponents of efforts to impose parental notification or consent requirements in federally funded programs. As these experts explained in a recent [June 18, 2003] letter to Congress:

> Most teens seeking services at [federally funded programs] are already sexually active. Mandating parental involvement is likely to discourage many teens from seeking family planning services, placing them at an increased risk for sexually transmitted diseases and unintended pregnancies. Studies indicate that one of the major causes of delay by adolescents in seeking contraception is fear of parental discovery and that many would avoid seeking services altogether if parental involvement were required.

Parental Consent Laws Do Not Improve Family Communication

The government cannot mandate healthy family communication. Federal law already requires health care providers in federally funded family planning clinics to encourage teenagers to talk to their parents about their health care decisions. Many teens, however, simply will not seek contraception if they cannot obtain it confidentially. Some justifiably fear that disclosure to their parents will lead to abandonment or abuse. Some simply have no caring and responsible parent to whom they can turn. Others live in families where sexuality is never openly discussed. As the New Jersey Supreme Court found [in *Planned Parenthood of Central New Jersey v. Farmer* (2002)], laws mandating parental involvement in teenagers' reproductive health care decisions "cannot transform a household with poor lines of communication into a paradigm of the perfect American family." Preventing teenagers from getting contraception unless they talk to a parent won't magically change these families; it will just result in teens having unprotected and unsafe sex.

Parental Consent Laws Violate Teens' Rights

The United States Constitution protects a minor's right to privacy in obtaining contraceptives. In *Carey v. Population Services International* [1977], the Supreme Court relied on minors' privacy rights to invalidate a New York law that prohibited the sale of condoms to adolescents under 16. The Court concluded that the "right to privacy in connection with decisions affecting procreation extends to minors as well as adults."

The Court held that the state interest in discouraging adolescents' sexual activity was not furthered by withholding from them the means to protect themselves. As Justice John Paul Stevens explained, to deny teenagers access to contraception in an effort to impress upon them the evils of underage sex is as irrational as if "a State decided to dramatize its disapproval of motorcycles by forbidding the use of safety helmets." The Constitution forbids this kind of "government-mandated harm."

Following the principles articulated in *Carey*, lower courts have invalidated parental involvement requirements for contraception. In *Planned Parenthood Association v. Matheson* [1983], for example, a federal district court recognized that teenagers' "'decisions whether to accomplish or prevent conception are among the most private and sensitive,'" and concluded that "the state may not impose a blanket parental notification requirement on minors seeking to exercise their constitutionally protected right to decide whether to bear or beget a child by using contraceptives."

In addition to minors' constitutional rights, two of the most important sources of federal family planning funds in the nation—Title X [Family Planning Program] and Medicaid—mandate confidentiality for teenagers seeking contraceptive services in those programs. Federal courts have consistently ruled that parental consent and notification requirements impermissibly conflict with this mandate.

Moreover, virtually every state has passed laws permitting teenagers to obtain care for STDs without involving a parent and most have express legal provisions guaranteeing confidential access to contraceptives as well. Even in those states without express laws, teens still have a constitutional right to access confidential care. Forced parental involvement would represent a dangerous reversal of longstanding public health policies.

> "My parents, being extremely conservative, would flip out if they even suspected I was having sex. So, I wanted birth control that was effective and confidential."

A Teen Decides to Seek Contraception Without Talking to Her Parents

Personal Narrative

Anonymous

In the following viewpoint, a seventeen-year-old girl explains the reasons she sought injections of the birth-control drug Depo-Provera. She maintains that she would feel more comfortable choosing to have sex if she would be protected from unintended pregnancy. She also reveals that for her, this was a private decision that she did not wish to share with her parents.

I've been in relationships before, but never felt ready for sex. Whether it was because of my boyfriend or me, sex was never something I wanted to do. Don't get me wrong, the temptation presented itself, but I'd never given it more than a short thought.

Anonymous, "How I Got 'the Shot,'" *Sex, Etc.*, May 4, 2002. www.sexetc.org. Copyright © 2002 by Answer. All rights reserved. Reproduced by permission.

Even though my religion says sex is for marriage, I think sex should be for love. I love my boyfriend, and I was the one to bring up sex. After ten months together, he'd never pressured me into anything. When we finally discussed sex, he made it clear that he was happy with us not having it.

Once I decided to have it, he repeatedly told me that if I changed my mind, he was OK with it. But I knew that whatever happens with us in the future, I wouldn't regret my decision.

Getting Protected

I knew that before I'd even consider actually having sex, I'd need to be on birth control. I refuse to risk becoming pregnant. My town is fortunate enough to have a clinic where teens can go for confidential birth control. A week after "the talk" with my boyfriend, I called the clinic and made an appointment.

Before I went, I decided to do some homework on birth control. My parents, being extremely conservative, would flip out if they even suspected I was having sex. So, I wanted birth control that was effective and confidential. That's why I decided to ask for Depo-Provera, also known as "the shot."

Depo-Provera is a prescription injection you get every three months. It contains a hormone similar to the chemical progesterone, which is found naturally in the female body. Like other forms of hormonal birth control, Depo-Provera prevents ovulation (the release of a female's egg from her ovaries), therefore making fertilization and pregnancy almost impossible.

The most common side effect of Depo-Provera is irregular menstrual bleeding. A female might have spotting between periods. Her periods may also become slightly heavier or lighter and less frequent. Many women on Depo eventually stop having periods while on it. Other possible side effects include slight weight gain, breast swelling or tenderness, stomachache, headache, or depression.

Despite all these, what attracted me so much to Depo is that it's more than 99-percent effective and incredibly simple. Only one shot every three months does the trick. And since it's an injection, it's hard for anyone to know you're on it. Privacy was important to me, since I can't imagine the scene if my parents found a pack of birth control pills in my purse.

Visiting a Clinic for the First Time

My boyfriend came with me to the clinic for emotional support. Although I wasn't exactly scared, I'd been nervous the entire day.

Since it was my first visit to the clinic, I had to spend about 20 minutes filling out forms about my health history, ways to be contacted, etc. When I finished, I went with a petite nurse into a small office. She introduced herself and, together, we discussed

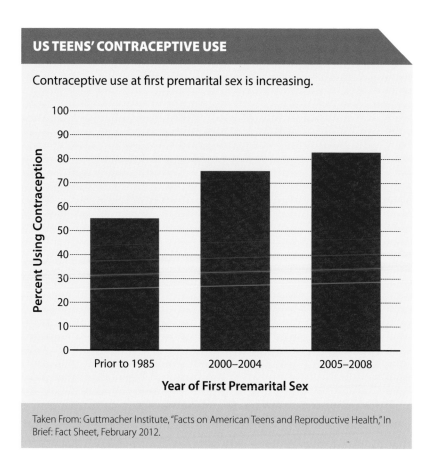

US TEENS' CONTRACEPTIVE USE

Contraceptive use at first premarital sex is increasing.

Taken From: Guttmacher Institute, "Facts on American Teens and Reproductive Health," In Brief: Fact Sheet, February 2012.

my history, my decision to have sex, and my birth control options.

Because I do not have unusual vaginal bleeding or a history of breast cancer, stroke, blood clots, or liver disease, the nurse agreed that Depo-Provera was a good choice, along with condoms—since Depo-Provera, like all other types of hormonal birth control, DOESN'T provide protection against sexually transmitted diseases.

The nurse informed me that, in addition to the visit cost, the shot is $35. We set up an appointment for the following week and she gave me a pile of pamphlets to read about Depo.

My boyfriend and I looked over the information and discussed our decision some more. The next week, I went back to the clinic to get the shot.

Getting the First Shot

A different nurse greeted me this time, but she was already familiar with my records and immediately put me at ease. I read and signed a consent form while she asked if I had any more questions. The form stated that I was aware of the possible side effects of the shot and that I would notify the clinic if I experienced anything abnormal.

There are two places on the body most women get the shot: the arm and the upper buttocks/lower back. I asked the nurse which one hurt less. She said the upper buttocks, because most women have more fat on the lower back, so it's usually less sore afterwards.

I listened to her advice and—with a small pinch that lasted about three seconds—I became protected against pregnancy for three months. (Depo works immediately when a female gets the shot within the first five days of her period.)

Eliminating the Worry of Pregnancy

I was amazed at how simple it all was, and I'm extremely happy that I chose Depo-Provera. My boyfriend and I also consistently use latex condoms, since the clinic advised that we practice two methods of birth control (to also protect against STDs).

My nurses were friendly and helpful and didn't make me feel as if my decision was something to be ashamed about. Rather, they felt that it was responsible of me to start birth control before I began having sex.

If the cost of birth control is an issue to anyone having sex, consider this: it's much cheaper to prevent a pregnancy than to pay for one. Also, most clinics (including Planned Parenthood health centers) have sliding-scale fees, meaning that you pay only what you can afford.

Going to the clinic took less than two hours out of my life, but it took the worry of getting pregnant out of my mind. Now that's a good deal.

NORTH ARKANSAS COLLEGE LIBRARY
1515 Pioneer Drive
Harrison, AR 72601

> "Women . . . suffer disproportionately
> the profound physical, emotional,
> and psychological consequences of
> sexual activity. The statute at issue
> here protects women . . . when those
> consequences are particularly severe."

Laws Targeting Men as the Perpetrators of Statutory Rape Are Just

The US Supreme Court's Decision

William Rehnquist

In 1981 the US Supreme Court upheld the constitutionality of a statute that declared it rape for men to have sex with someone under the age of eighteen but did not consider the potential for women to be criminally liable as well. Michael M., a seventeen year old, challenged the law after being accused of raping a sixteen-year-old girl. He claimed that he could not be charged because the gender bias deprived him of equal protection. The California courts insisted the law was permissible because it served to reduce teen pregnancy. The US Supreme Court agreed, stating the law was constitutional given the importance of the state government's objectives. William Rehnquist served as an associate justice of the US Supreme Court from 1972 to 1986 and then as chief justice from 1986 to 2005.

William Rehnquist, Plurality opinion, *Michael M. v. Superior Court of Sonoma County*, US Supreme Court, March 23, 1981.

The question presented in this case is whether California's "statutory rape" law, 261.5 of the Cal. Penal Code Ann., violates the Equal Protection Clause of the Fourteenth Amendment. Section 261.5 defines unlawful sexual intercourse as "an act of sexual intercourse accomplished with a female not the wife of the perpetrator, where the female is under the age of 18 years." The statute thus makes men alone criminally liable for the act of sexual intercourse.

In July 1978, a complaint was filed in the Municipal Court of Sonoma County, Cal., alleging that petitioner, then a 17 1/2-year-old male, had unlawful sexual intercourse with a female under the age of 18, in violation of 261.5. The evidence adduced at a preliminary hearing showed that at approximately midnight on June 3, 1978, petitioner and two friends approached Sharon, a 16 1/2-year-old female, and her sister as they waited at a bus stop. Petitioner and Sharon, who had already been drinking, moved away from the others and began to kiss. After being struck in the face for rebuffing petitioner's initial advances, Sharon submitted to sexual intercourse with petitioner. Prior to trial, petitioner sought to set aside the information on both state and federal constitutional grounds, asserting that 261.5 unlawfully discriminated on the basis of gender. The trial court and the California Court of Appeal denied petitioner's request for relief and petitioner sought review in the Supreme Court of California.

The State Has a Compelling Interest in Preventing Teen Pregnancy

The Supreme Court held that "section 261.5 discriminates on the basis of sex because only females may be victims, and only males may violate the section." The court then subjected the classification to "strict scrutiny," stating that it must be justified by a compelling state interest. It found that the classification was "supported not by mere social convention but by the immutable physiological fact that it is the female exclusively who can become pregnant." Canvassing "the tragic human costs of illegitimate teenage pregnancies," including the large number of teenage abortions, the increased medical risk associated with teenage pregnancies, and the social consequences of teenage childbearing, the court concluded that the State has a compelling interest

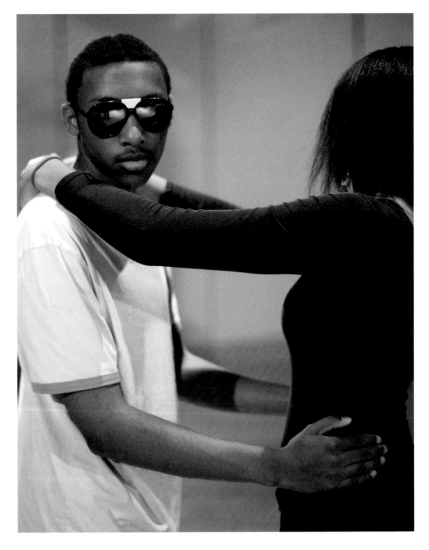

Despite the fact that sexual activity may be consensual between teens, the US Supreme Court places the burden of punishment on the boy, arguing that he alone can cause a pregnancy to occur. © Hill Street Studios/Getty Images.

in preventing such pregnancies. Because males alone can "physiologically cause the result which the law properly seeks to avoid," the court further held that the gender classification was readily justified as a means of identifying offender and victim. For the reasons stated below, we affirm the judgment of the California Supreme Court.

As is evident from our opinions, the Court has had some difficulty in agreeing upon the proper approach and analysis in cases involving challenges to gender-based classifications. The issues posed by such challenges range from issues of standing to the appropriate standard of judicial review for the substantive classification. Unlike the California Supreme Court, we have not held that gender-based classifications are "inherently suspect" and thus we do not apply so-called "strict scrutiny" to those classifications. Our cases have held, however, that the traditional minimum rationality test takes on a somewhat "sharper focus" when gender-based classifications are challenged. In *Reed v. Reed* (1971), for example, the Court stated that a gender-based classification will be upheld if it bears a "fair and substantial relationship" to legitimate state ends, while in *Craig v. Boren* [1976], the Court restated the test to require the classification to bear a "substantial relationship" to "important governmental objectives."

Circumstances Permit Gendered Laws

Underlying these decisions is the principle that a legislature may not "make overbroad generalizations based on sex which are entirely unrelated to any differences between men and women or which demean the ability or social status of the affected class." *Parham v. Hughes* (1979). But because the Equal Protection Clause does not "demand that a statute necessarily apply equally to all persons" or require "'things which are different in fact . . . to be treated in law as though they were the same,'" *Rinaldi v. Yeager* (1966), this Court has consistently upheld statutes where the gender classification is not invidious, but rather realistically reflects the fact that the sexes are not similarly situated in certain circumstances. As the Court has stated, a legislature may "provide for the special problems of women." *Weinberger v. Wiesenfeld* (1975).

Applying those principles to this case, the fact that the California Legislature criminalized the act of illicit sexual intercourse with a minor female is a sure indication of its intent or purpose to discourage that conduct. Precisely why the legislature desired that result is of course somewhat less clear. This Court has long recognized that "[i]nquiries into congressional motives or purposes are a hazardous matter," *United States v. O'Brien* (1968). Here, for example, the individual legislators may have voted for the statute for a variety of reasons. Some legislators may have been concerned about preventing teenage pregnancies, others about protecting young females from physical injury or from the loss of "chastity," and still others about promoting various religious and moral attitudes towards premarital sex.

The justification for the statute offered by the State, and accepted by the Supreme Court of California, is that the legislature sought to prevent illegitimate teenage pregnancies. That finding, of course, is entitled to great deference. And although our cases establish that the State's asserted reason for the enactment of a statute may be rejected, if it "could not have been a goal of the legislation," *Weinberger v. Wiesenfeld*, this is not such a case.

The State Has a Constitutional Right to Seek the Reduction of Teen Pregnancy

We are satisfied not only that the prevention of illegitimate pregnancy is at least one of the "purposes" of the statute, but also that the State has a strong interest in preventing such pregnancy. At the risk of stating the obvious, teenage pregnancies, which have increased dramatically over the last two decades, have significant social, medical, and economic consequences for both the mother and her child, and the State. Of particular concern to the State is that approximately half of all teenage pregnancies end in

The Hazard of Consent-Based Standards for Statutory Rape Laws

As a result of moving to a consent-based standard in the enforcement of statutory rape laws, modern criminal law has turned girls from "jail bait" into "fair game" without considering the nature and meaning of consensual sexual activity for girls, or whether any of the factors that might induce consent should be legally impermissible. The presumption underlying modern law governing adolescent girls' sexuality is that girls are mature enough to make autonomous decisions regarding sexuality. However, the growing body of research on female adolescence calls into question the presumption that girls are fully capable of protecting themselves. That is, researchers consistently have found that for girls, adolescence is a time of acute crisis, in which self-esteem, body image, academic confidence, and the willingness to speak out decline precipitously. Such evidence reveals a significant likelihood that girls are vulnerable in sexual encounters—vulnerable in precisely the manner which the common law of statutory rape anticipated and sought to remedy.

Michelle Oberman, "Turning Girls into Women:
Re-evaluating Modern Statutory Rape Laws,"
Journal of Criminal Law and Criminology,
June 22, 1994.

abortion. And of those children who are born, their illegitimacy makes them likely candidates to become wards of the State.

We need not be medical doctors to discern that young men and young women are not similarly situated with respect to the problems and the risks of sexual intercourse. Only women may become pregnant, and they suffer disproportionately the profound physical, emotional, and psychological consequences of sexual activity. The statute at issue here protects women from sexual intercourse at an age when those consequences are particularly severe.

The question thus boils down to whether a State may attack the problem of sexual intercourse and teenage pregnancy directly by prohibiting a male from having sexual intercourse with a minor female. We hold that such a statute is sufficiently related to the State's objectives to pass constitutional muster.

Because virtually all of the significant harmful and inescapably identifiable consequences of teenage pregnancy fall on the young female, a legislature acts well within its authority when it elects to punish only the participant who, by nature, suffers few of the consequences of his conduct. It is hardly unreasonable for a legislature acting to protect minor females to exclude them from punishment. Moreover, the risk of pregnancy itself constitutes a substantial deterrence to young females. No similar natural sanctions deter males. A criminal sanction imposed solely on males thus serves to roughly "equalize" the deterrents on the sexes.

The Petitioner's Arguments Are Unpersuasive

We are unable to accept petitioner's contention that the statute is impermissibly underinclusive and must, in order to pass judicial scrutiny, be broadened so as to hold the female as criminally liable as the male. It is argued that this statute is not necessary to deter teenage pregnancy because a gender-neutral statute, where both male and female would be subject to prosecution, would serve that goal equally well. The relevant inquiry, however, is not whether the statute is drawn as precisely as it might have been, but whether the line chosen by the California Legislature is within constitutional limitations.

In any event, we cannot say that a gender-neutral statute would be as effective as the statute California has chosen to enact. The State persuasively contends that a gender-neutral statute would frustrate its interest in effective enforcement. Its view is that a female is surely less likely to report violations of the statute if she herself would be subject to criminal prosecution. In an area already fraught with prosecutorial difficulties, we decline to hold that the Equal Protection Clause requires a legislature to enact a statute so broad that it may well be incapable of enforcement.

We similarly reject petitioner's argument that 261.5 is impermissibly overbroad because it makes unlawful sexual intercourse with prepubescent females, who are, by definition, incapable of becoming pregnant. Quite apart from the fact that the statute could well be justified on the grounds that very young females are particularly susceptible to physical injury from sexual intercourse, it is ludicrous to suggest that the Constitution requires the California Legislature to limit the scope of its rape statute to older teenagers and exclude young girls.

There remains only petitioner's contention that the statute is unconstitutional as it is applied to him because he, like Sharon, was under 18 at the time of sexual intercourse. Petitioner argues that the statute is flawed because it presumes that as between two persons under 18, the male is the culpable aggressor. We find petitioner's contentions unpersuasive. Contrary to his assertions, the statute does not rest on the assumption that males are generally the aggressors. It is instead an attempt by a legislature to prevent illegitimate teenage pregnancy by providing an additional deterrent for men. The age of the man is irrelevant since young men are as capable as older men of inflicting the harm sought to be prevented.

In upholding the California statute we also recognize that this is not a case where a statute is being challenged on the grounds that it "invidiously discriminates" against females. To the contrary, the statute places a burden on males which is not shared by females. But we find nothing to suggest that men, because of past discrimination or peculiar disadvantages, are in need of the special solicitude of the courts. Nor is this a case where the gender classification is made "solely for . . . administrative convenience," as in *Frontiero v. Richardson* (1973) or rests on "the baggage of sexual stereotypes" as in *Orr v. Orr* [1979]. As we have held, the statute instead reasonably reflects the fact that the consequences of sexual intercourse and pregnancy fall more heavily on the female than on the male.

| "Common sense . . . suggests that a gender-neutral statutory rape law is potentially a greater deterrent of sexual activity than a gender-based law."

Laws Targeting Men as the Perpetrators of Statutory Rape Are Unconstitutional

Dissenting Opinion

William J. Brennan

In 1978, Michael M., a seventeen-year-old male, was charged with rape under a California statute after having sex with a sixteen-year-old girl who resisted his advances. The statute was worded solely to indict men who had sex with women under the age of eighteen. Michael M. claimed the law deprived him of equal protection because of its gender bias. Michael M. v. Superior Court of Sonoma County *(1981) reached the US Supreme Court, and the court upheld the statute, claiming that California had compelling reason to keep the law intact. In the following viewpoint, a US Supreme Court justice dissents from the prevailing ruling, stating that the state failed to show a gendered law was more effective at reducing teen pregnancy than a gender-neutral law that sought the*

William J. Brennan, Dissenting opinion, *Michael M. v. Superior Court of Sonoma County*, US Supreme Court, March 23, 1981.

same goal. He maintains the law is based on outdated stereotypes and violates equal protection rights set forth in the Fourteenth Amendment. William J. Brennan served as an associate justice of the US Supreme Court from 1956 to 1990.

It is disturbing to find the Court so splintered on a case that presents such a straightforward issue: Whether the admittedly gender-based classification in Cal. Penal Code Ann. 261.5 bears a sufficient relationship to the State's asserted goal of preventing teenage pregnancies to survive the "mid-level" constitutional scrutiny mandated by *Craig v. Boren* (1976). Applying the analytical framework provided by our precedents, I am convinced that there is only one proper resolution of this issue: the classification must be declared unconstitutional. I fear that the plurality opinion and Justice [Potter] Stewart and [Harry] Blackmun reach the opposite result by placing too much emphasis on the desirability of achieving the State's asserted statutory goal—prevention of teenage pregnancy—and not enough emphasis on the fundamental question of whether the sex-based discrimination in the California statute is substantially related to the achievement of that goal.

After some uncertainty as to the proper framework for analyzing equal protection challenges to statutes containing gender-based classifications, this Court settled upon the proposition that a statute containing a gender-based classification cannot withstand constitutional challenge unless the classification is substantially related to the achievement of an important governmental objective. This analysis applies whether the classification discriminates against males or against females. The burden is on the government to prove both the importance of its asserted objective and the substantial relationship between the classification and that objective. And the State cannot meet that burden without showing that a gender-neutral statute would be a less effective means of achieving that goal.

The State of California vigorously asserts that the "important governmental objective" to be served by 261.5 is the prevention of teenage pregnancy. It claims that its statute furthers this goal by deterring sexual activity by males—the class of persons it considers more responsible for causing those pregnancies. But even assuming that prevention of teenage pregnancy is an important governmental objective and that it is in fact an objective of 261.5, California still has the burden of proving that there are fewer teenage pregnancies under its gender-based statutory rape law than there would be if the law were gender neutral. To meet this burden, the State must show that because its statutory rape law punishes only males, and not females, it more effectively deters minor females from having sexual intercourse.

The plurality assumes that a gender-neutral statute would be less effective than 261.5 in deterring sexual activity because a gender-neutral statute would create significant enforcement problems. The plurality thus accepts the State's assertion that:

US Supreme Court Justices Harry Blackmun, William J. Brennan, and John Paul Stevens (left to right) speak at a Washington, DC, church in 1987. Brennan wrote the dissenting opinion in the case of Michael M. v. Superior Court of Sonoma County, *citing its gender bias.* © AP Images/Bob Daugherty.

a female is surely less likely to report violations of the statute if she herself would be subject to criminal prosecution. In an area already fraught with prosecutorial difficulties, we decline to hold that the Equal Protection Clause requires a legislature to enact a statute so broad that it may well be incapable of enforcement.

The State's Argument Is Flawed

However, a State's bare assertion that its gender-based statutory classification substantially furthers an important governmental interest is not enough to meet its burden of proof under *Craig v. Boren*. Rather, the State must produce evidence that will persuade the court that its assertion is true.

The State has not produced such evidence in this case. Moreover, there are at least two serious flaws in the State's assertion that law enforcement problems created by a gender-neutral statutory rape law would make such a statute less effective than a gender-based statute in deterring sexual activity.

First, the experience of other jurisdictions, and California itself, belies the plurality's conclusion that a gender-neutral statutory rape law "may well be incapable of enforcement." There are now at least 37 States that have enacted gender-neutral statutory rape laws. Although most of these laws protect young persons (of either sex) from the sexual exploitation of older individuals, the laws of Arizona, Florida, and Illinois permit prosecution of both minor females and minor males for engaging in mutual sexual conduct. California has introduced no evidence that those States have been handicapped by the enforcement problems the plurality finds so persuasive. Surely, if those States could provide such evidence, we might expect that California would have introduced it.

In addition, the California Legislature in recent years has revised other sections of the Penal Code to make them gender-neutral. For example, Cal. Penal Code Ann. 286 (b) (1) and 288a (b)(i), prohibiting sodomy and oral copulation with a "person who is under 18 years of age," could cause two minor homosexuals to be subjected to criminal sanctions for engaging in mutually consensual conduct. Again, the State has introduced no evidence to explain why a gender-neutral statutory rape law would be any more difficult to enforce than those statutes.

The second flaw in the State's assertion is that even assuming that a gender-neutral statute would be more difficult to enforce, the State has still not shown that those enforcement problems would make such a statute less effective than a gender-based statute in deterring minor females from engaging in sexual intercourse. Common sense, however, suggests that a gender-neutral statutory rape law is potentially a greater deterrent of sexual activity than a gender-based law, for the simple reason that a gender-neutral law subjects both men and women to criminal sanctions and thus arguably has a deterrent effect on twice as many potential violators. Even if fewer persons were prosecuted under the gender-neutral law, as the State suggests, it would still be true that twice as many persons would be subject to arrest. The State's failure to prove that a gender-neutral law would be a less effective deterrent than a gender-based law, like the State's failure to prove that a gender-neutral law would be difficult to enforce, should have led this Court to invalidate 261.5.

The Gender-Based Law Was Built on Sexual Stereotypes

Until very recently, no California court or commentator had suggested that the purpose of California's statutory rape law was to protect young women from the risk of pregnancy. Indeed, the historical development of 261.5 demonstrates that the law was initially enacted on the premise that young women, in contrast to young men, were to be deemed legally incapable of consenting to an act of sexual intercourse. Because their chastity was considered particularly precious, those young women were felt to be uniquely in need of the State's protection. In contrast, young men were assumed to be capable of making such decisions for

Gender-Based Rape Laws Create a Double Standard

Legal scholars have also . . . convincingly argued that gendered statutory rape laws evidence a double standard of sexual morality. Simply stated, the law's protection of females and not of males reflects the belief that "female sexual morals" should be restricted more than "male sexual morals." Furthermore, the sexual double standard and gendered laws validate and reinforce each other, because both rest on and preserve pernicious sex role stereotypes. This argument comprises several components. First, the protection of only women legitimates the notion that young women are, [according to researcher Marsha Greenfield] "by nature, noble and pure and therefore to be protected from immoral activity." According to this model, because young women are passive and ignorant, they are more vulnerable to emotional, physical, and social harm resulting from sexual intercourse. Secondly, by qualifying only young females for victim status, gendered statutory rape laws presume that minor females, unlike minor males, are incapable of understanding the nature and consequences of sexual intercourse. Gender-based statutory rape laws thus embody and reinforce a stereotypical idea that girls are intellectually deficient and incompetent in a way that boys are not.

Kay L. Levine, "No Penis, No Problem,"
Fordham Urban Law Journal, *2006.*

themselves; the law therefore did not offer them any special protection.

It is perhaps because the gender classification in California's statutory rape law was initially designed to further these outmoded sexual stereotypes, rather than to reduce the incidence of teenage pregnancies, that the State has been unable to demonstrate a substantial relationship between the classification and its newly asserted goal. But whatever the reason, the State has not shown that Cal. Penal Code 261.5 is any more effective than a gender-neutral law would be in deterring minor females from engaging in sexual intercourse. It has therefore not met its burden of proving that the statutory classification is substantially related to the achievement of its asserted goal.

I would hold that 261.5 violates the Equal Protection Clause of the Fourteenth Amendment, and I would reverse the judgment of the California Supreme Court.

| "When two children under the age of 13 engage in sexual conduct with each other, each child is both an offender and a victim."

A Child Thirteen or Younger Cannot Be Charged with Statutory Rape for Sex with Peers in Most Cases

The Ohio Supreme Court's Decision

Judith Ann Lanzinger

In 2007, the state of Ohio filed complaints against a thirteen-year-old boy, D.B., for allegedly using force to engage in sexual activity with an eleven-year-old boy, M.G., and a twelve-year-old boy, A.W. The state charged that D.B. committed rape under a state statute that holds offenders liable for sex with persons under thirteen years old. D.B. argued that the statute was unconstitutional because he was also a member of the group the law protected. In the following viewpoint, an Ohio Supreme Court justice asserts that the law was clear when the offending party is an adult but not when all people involved are thirteen or under. The author maintains that all the children were liable as offenders and protected as

Judith Ann Lanzinger, Opinion of the Court, *In re D.B.*, Supreme Court of Ohio, June 8, 2011.

victims, thus affirming that the statute in question was unconstitutional. Judith Ann Lanzinger was elected to the Supreme Court of Ohio in 2004.

R.C. 2907.02(A)(1)(b) criminalizes what is commonly known as "statutory rape." The statute holds offenders strictly liable for engaging in sexual conduct with children under the age of 13—force is not an element of the offense because a child under the age of 13 is legally presumed to be incapable of consenting to sexual conduct.

The Scope of the Statutory Rape Law

R.C. 2907.02(A)(1) provides:

"No person shall engage in sexual conduct with another who is not the spouse of the offender or who is the spouse of the offender but is living separate and apart from the offender, when any of the following applies: . . .

"(b) The other person is less than 13 years of age, whether or not the offender knows the age of the other person."

The statute furthers the state's interest in protecting young children. Indeed, the Legislature Service Commission stated that R.C. 2907.02(A)(1)(b) was created to protect a prepubescent child from the sexual advances of another because "engaging in sexual conduct with such a person indicates vicious behavior on the part of the offender."

D.B. argues that R.C. 2907.02(A)(1)(b) is unconstitutional in two ways. First, he argues that the statute is vague as applied to children under the age of 13 and thus violates his right to due process. Second, he argues that the statute was applied in an arbitrary manner in this case in contravention of his constitutional right to equal protection. This case thus asks whether a child's federal constitutional rights are violated when, as a member of the class protected under R.C. 2907.02(A)(1)(b), he or she is adjudicated delinquent based upon a violation of this statute.

The Challenge to Due Process

D.B. argues that R.C. 2907.02(A)(1)(b) is unconstitutional as applied to him because it fails to provide guidelines that designate which actor is the victim and which is the offender, resulting in arbitrary and discriminatory enforcement.

"It is fundamental that a court must 'presume the constitutionality of lawfully enacted legislation.'" *Arnold v. Cleveland* (1993). Accordingly, the legislation in question "will not be invalidated unless the challenger establishes that it is unconstitutional beyond a reasonable doubt."

Juvenile delinquency hearings "must measure up to the essentials of due process and fair treatment." *In re Gault* (1967). Due process is not satisfied if a statute is unconstitutionally vague. *Skilling v. United States* (2010). "A statute can be impermissibly vague for either of two independent reasons. First, if it fails to provide people of ordinary intelligence a reasonable opportunity to understand what conduct it prohibits. Second, if it authorizes or even encourages arbitrary and discriminatory enforcement." *Chicago v. Morales* (1999). . . .

Aspects of the Law Are Unconstitutionally Vague

As applied to children under the age of 13 who engage in sexual conduct with other children under the age of 13, R.C. 2907.02(A)(1)(b) is unconstitutionally vague because the statute authorizes and encourages arbitrary and discriminatory enforcement. When an adult engages in sexual conduct with a child under the age of 13, it is clear which party is the offender and which is the victim. But when two children under the age of 13 engage in sexual conduct with each other, each child is both an offender and a victim, and the distinction between those two terms breaks down.

The facts of this case provide an example of the temptation for prosecutors to label one child as the offender and the other child as the victim. Based apparently upon the theory that D.B. forced

An adolescent couple chats intimately in their school hallway. The Ohio Supreme Court ruled that children under the age of thirteen are legally incapable of granting sexual consent and therefore cannot be charged with statutory rape. © Laurence Mouton/Getty Images.

M.G. to engage in sexual conduct, the state alleged that D.B., but not M.G., had engaged in conduct that constituted statutory rape. However, while the theory of D.B. as the aggressor was consistent with the counts alleging a violation of R.C. 2907.02(A)(2), which proscribes rape by force, this theory is incompatible with the counts alleging a violation of statutory rape because anyone who engages in sexual conduct with a minor under the age of 13 commits statutory rape regardless of whether force was used. Thus, if the facts alleged in the complaint were true, D.B. and M.G. would both be in violation of R.C. 2907.02(A)(1)(b).

The prosecutor's choice to charge D.B. but not M.G. is the very definition of discriminatory enforcement. D.B. and M.G. engaged in sexual conduct with each other, yet only D.B. was charged. The facts of this case demonstrate that R.C. 2907.02(A)(1)(b) authorizes and encourages arbitrary and discriminatory enforcement when applied to offenders under the age of 13. The statute is thus unconstitutionally vague as applied to this situation.

It must be emphasized that the concept of consent plays no role in whether a person violates R.C. 2907.02(A)(1)(b): children under the age of 13 are legally incapable of consenting to sexual conduct. Furthermore, whether D.B. used force to engage in sexual conduct does not play a role in our consideration of R.C. 2907.02(A)(1)(b). The trial court found that D.B. did not use force. Whether an offender used force is irrelevant to the determination whether the offender committed rape under R.C. 2907.02(A)(1)(b).

We note that while we hold that R.C. 2907.02(A)(1)(b) is unconstitutional as applied to a child under the age of 13 who engages in sexual conduct with another child under the age of 13, a child under the age of 13 may be found guilty of rape if additional elements are shown: the offender substantially impairs the other person's judgment or control, R.C. 2907.02(A)(1)(a); the other person's ability to resist or consent is substantially impaired because of a mental or physical condition, R.C. 2907.02(A)(1)(c);

A Constitutional Challenge That May Not Prevail for Long

> Because of the scope of this ruling, because it is such a departure from the traditional view of prosecutorial power [which seeks to assign blame to one party], and because it is done by a state supreme court in the name of the U.S. Constitution and not just of the state constitution, I'm inclined to think that there's a substantial probability that the U.S. Supreme Court will hear the case. And if it does, I think most of the Justices will vote to reverse.
>
> *Eugene Volokh, "Statutory Rape Laws Held Unconstitutionally Open to Selective Enforcement, as Applied to Sex Between Two Minors,"* Volokh Conspiracy, *June 9, 2011. www.volokh.com.*

or the offender compels the other person to submit by force or threat of force, R.C. 2907.02(A)(2). None of those additional elements was present here.

The Statute Violates Equal Protection Guarantees

Application of R.C. 2907.02(A)(1)(b) in this case also violates D.B.'s federal right to equal protection. "The Equal Protection Clause directs that 'all persons similarly circumstanced shall be treated alike.'" *F.S. Royster Guano Co. v. Virginia* (1920).

The plain language of the statute makes it clear that every person who engages in sexual conduct with a child under the age of 13 is strictly liable for statutory rape, and the statute must be enforced equally and without regard to the particular circumstances of an individual's situation. R.C. 2907.02(A)(1)(b) offers no prosecutorial exception to charging an offense when every party involved in the sexual conduct is under the age of 13;

conceivably, the principle of equal protection suggests that both parties could be prosecuted as identically situated. Because D.B. and M.G. were both under the age of 13 at the time the events in this case occurred, they were both members of the class protected by the statute, and both could have been charged under the offense. Application of the statute in this case to a single party violates the Equal Protection Clause's mandate that persons similarly circumstanced shall be treated alike.

All three boys allegedly engaged in sexual conduct with a person under the age of 13; however, only D.B. was charged with a violation of R.C. 2907.02(A)(1)(b). This arbitrary enforcement of the statute violates D.B.'s right to equal protection. We accordingly hold that application of the statute in this case violated D.B.'s federal equal-protection rights. The statute is unconstitutional as applied to him.

The Statute Is Unconstitutional

R.C. 2907.02(A)(1)(b) prohibits one from engaging in sexual conduct with a person under the age of 13. As applied to offenders who are under the age of 13 themselves, the statute is unconstitutionally vague in violation of the Due Process Clause of the United States Constitution because arbitrary and discriminatory enforcement is encouraged. Application of the statute in this case also violates the Equal Protection Clause of the United States Constitution because only one child was charged with being delinquent, while others similarly situated were not.

We thus hold that R.C. 2907.02(A)(1)(b) is unconstitutional as applied to a child under the age of 13 who engages in sexual conduct with another child under 13.

> "It is . . . our responsibility as adults
> to think critically ourselves about the
> benefits and risks of the laws we make
> and how we apply them."

Age of Consent Laws Are Inconsistent and Rely on Outdated Stereotypes of Masculinity and Femininity

Martha Kempner

In the following viewpoint, a sexual rights advocate provides a brief history about age of consent laws, noting how they have changed over the centuries. The author also discusses how modern consent and statutory rape laws in the United States vary from state to state and even differ within states as to what constitutes illegal sexual behavior. She believes these laws are often unjust because they ignore consensual sexual relations in order to prosecute against predatory conduct, and they rely on outdated stereotypes of female victimhood and male aggressiveness. She worries that these laws can unfairly saddle young men with sex offender charges and keep young women away from sexual health services for fear of disclosing a potentially illegal relationship. Martha Kempner, a former

Martha Kempner, "Legislating Teen Sex: What's (Terribly) Wrong with Our Age of Consent Laws," *RH Reality Check*, March 27, 2012. www.rhrealitycheck.org. Copyright © 2012 by RH Reality Check. All rights reserved. Reproduced by permission.

vice president of the Sexuality Information and Education Council of the United States, writes and consults on sexual health topics.

Last month [February 2012], my husband forwarded me [an] article from the *Daily Beast* and I haven't been able to get it out of my mind since. The article focuses on a few young men who went to jail and wound up on sex offender registries ostensibly for having sex with their teenage girlfriends. While the young men were teenagers themselves, at 18 the law considered them adults whereas their girlfriends at 14 and 15 were under the legal age of consent. Now, in fairness, neither of these boys went to jail just for having sex with an underage girl, there were aggravating circumstances—one punched his girlfriend's father and both violated judges' orders to stay away from the girls.

Still, all I could think about was that what started out as a somewhat typical high school relationship (a senior boy with a freshman or sophomore girlfriend is not at all that unusual) essentially ruined these young men's lives. Not only did they spend time in jail and postpone any future plans, their names now sit on sex offender registries alongside those of serial rapist, child pornographers, and pedophiles.

Consensual Relationships Can Be Criminal

And as is human nature, all I could think about was my own life story. Once upon a time, a couple of decades ago or so, I was in one of those not unusual relationships between a sophomore girl and a senior boy. In true high school style, we were fixed up by friends at the beginning of my sophomore year and had an on-again-off-again flirtation throughout the fall and winter (too much of which involved me watching from a distance as his relationship with a perky senior named Suzanne played out in the halls between classes). But by spring they had broken up and one fateful Wednesday he called. From there we began what would be my first serious and my first sexual relationship.

By the time we had sex, we had been together for many months and professed our love for each other. I had nursed him back to puffy-cheeked health after he'd had his wisdom teeth out and he had spent a great deal of time with my family on Cape Cod. Though I can't say it was a perfect relationship or the balance of power was entirely equal (he held some advantage by virtue of being older and more experienced), I can assure you that the sexual aspect of our relationship was consensual, mutually pleasurable, non-exploitative, honest, and protected from pregnancy and STDs. (Years later as a sexuality educator, these are among the litmus tests I would suggest to teens.)

The problem that really didn't occur to me until last week, however, is that from a legal standpoint it was not a consensual relationship. In Massachusetts—which has one of the least nuanced laws regarding age of consent—a person under 16 cannot give consent, and I was three months shy of my 16th birthday that summer. So, though I saw it as a normal and mostly positive sexual experience, had authorities been notified of it for whatever reason, they would have declared it a crime.

This realization had my head swimming with questions. Should we really treat teenagers who have sex with other teenagers as criminals? Should our legal system play any role in regulating "consensual" teen sexual behavior? Is there a way to protect teens from exploitation without making them vulnerable to unnecessary prosecution? And what does all of this say about how society handles teen sex?

The History of Statutory Rape Laws

Statutory rape laws (which are called by a plethora of other names) refer to those laws that "criminalize voluntary sexual acts involving a minor that would be legal if not for the age of one or more of the participants." The premise behind these laws is that until a certain age, young people are incapable of giving their consent for sexual behavior but the intent behind the laws has morphed over the 700 years or so since they were first codified. The first known law, passed in Westminster England in 1275, made it illegal to "ravish" a "maiden" under the age of 12 (also the age at which a girl could legally marry) without her consent. Later laws reduced this age to 10 or 11. The result was that an underage girl did not have to show that she had struggled in order to prove that she had not given her consent as her older friends did. Age of consent laws, therefore, made it easier to prosecute a man who sexually assaulted an underage girl. The acknowledged purpose of these laws was to protect the young girl's "chastity," possibly so as not to ruin her future chances for marriage.

Though they remained largely unchanged for several centuries, the laws began to morph in the late 1800s and early 1900s as other aspects of societies and the role of women changed. European nations and U.S. states slowly raised the age to 13 and 14 under scientific arguments that this is when young women begin to menstruate and reach physical maturity. In the 1920s and 30s as the modern concept of the teenager began to emerge and movements formed to fight child prostitution and exploitation, the age of consent in most states was raised to 16 or even 18.

Not everyone agreed with these changes, however. Some argued that teenage women "were sufficiently developed not to need legal protection," and, moreover, that "by late adolescence girls possessed sufficient understanding about how to use the law to blackmail unwary men." Steven Robertson of the University of Australia Sydney points out in an article that the term "jailbait," gained popularity in the 1930s because people recognized "teenage girls as sexually attractive, even sexually active, but legally unavailable."

Still, even if people acknowledged young women as sexual, [Robertson writes] the general consensus was that the laws were necessary to protect them from exploitation:

> . . . . in making it a crime for girls to decide to have sexual intercourse outside marriage, the law protected them from them-

selves and from the immature understanding that led them to behaviors reformers considered immoral.

Feminists of the 1970s agreed that it was important to protect young people from exploitation but worked to ensure that these laws did not "unduly restrict the sexual autonomy of young women." Part of this became efforts to make the laws gender-neutral and ensure an understanding of the rationale behind them:

Aiming to challenge stereotypes of female passivity and growing concern about male victimization, they made it clearer that the laws concerned all youth—male and female—and that the laws protected them from exploitation rather than ensuring their virginity.

During the debates over welfare reform in the mid-nineties—the same debates that brought us the federal government's increasing investment in abstinence-only-until-marriage programs—

A billboard in Michigan warns about the legal consequences of sex before the age of consent. Definitions of consent and sexual maturity have changed greatly over the past seven hundred years. Some argue that current laws are too strict and can ruin the lives of young people. © AP Images/Norma Lerner.

a new rationale for these laws was thrown about. Armed with the statistic that half the children born to adolescent women are fathered by adult men and that many of these children end up on welfare, some state and federal lawmakers began to argue that stricter enforcement of statutory rape laws would deter older men from having sex with teenage girls and would, therefore, solve the teen pregnancy problem. California invested millions of dollars into increasing the prosecution of such cases; Delaware passed the "Sexual Predator Act of 1996," and began "stationing state police in high schools to identify students who have become involved with adult men;" and Florida passed a law that declared "impregnation of a minor younger than age 16 by a male aged 21 or older" to be a reportable form of child abuse.

While some law enforcement officials thought this was the right approach, many advocates for adolescent health were skeptical at best. The deputy district attorney in California's Tulare County told the *L.A. Times*: "When we prosecute a few of these guys, we think it'll make a lot of guys think twice." By contrast, law professor Michelle Oberman felt these laws would never act as a deterrent:

> Drawing a connection between enforcing these laws and lowering adolescent pregnancy rates flies in the face of everything we know about why girls get pregnant and why they choose to continue their pregnancies. The problem is much more complicated than simply older men preying on younger women.

The argument about using age of consent laws to prevent teen pregnancy seems to have lost some of its momentum in recent years and the general consensus has returned to the idea that these laws remain important to protect young people (primarily young women) from exploitation. The question remains, however, how do these laws distinguish between exploitative relationships and consensual relationships between young people?

Confusing Terminology Across State Laws

The truth is that these laws cannot make such distinctions but lawmakers seem to have attempted to account for variations in relationships. The laws are certainly more nuanced than I had expected; though above anything else, these laws are complicated. Each state has its own law and decides a number of factors for itself, including age of consent, minimum age of "victim," age differential, and minimum age of "perpetrator" in order to prosecute.

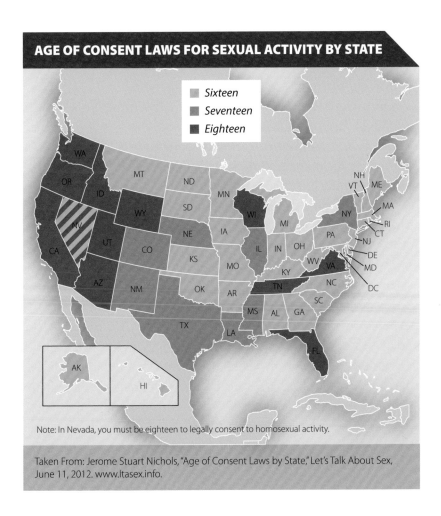

AGE OF CONSENT LAWS FOR SEXUAL ACTIVITY BY STATE

Sixteen
Seventeen
Eighteen

Note: In Nevada, you must be eighteen to legally consent to homosexual activity.

Taken From: Jerome Stuart Nichols, "Age of Consent Laws by State," Let's Talk About Sex, June 11, 2012. www.ltasex.info.

- *Age of consent.* This is the age at which an individual *can* legally consent to sexual intercourse under any circumstances.
- *Minimum age of victim.* This is the age below which an individual *cannot* legally consent to sexual intercourse under any circumstance.
- *Age differential.* If the victim is above the minimum age but below the age of consent, the age differential is the maximum age difference between the victim and the perpetrator where an individual *can* legally consent to sexual intercourse.
- *Minimum of age of defendant in order to prosecute.* This is the age below which an individual *cannot* be prosecuted for engaging in sexual activities with minors.

Anyone else confused by these distinctions?

Only 12 states have a single age of consent below which an individual cannot consent to sexual intercourse and above which they can. As I mentioned earlier, Massachusetts is one of those states—the age of consent there is simply 16. That leaves 39 other states where the laws are more complicated. I found that the only way I could follow them was to look at some specific examples. (These particular examples were spelled out in a report prepared for the U.S. Department of Health and Human Services in 2003 so there is possibility that some laws have changed since.)

In most states, the law takes into account both the age of the victim and the difference in ages between the victim and the perpetrator. In my home state of New Jersey, for example, the age of consent is 16 but "individuals who are at least 13 years of age can legally engage in sexual activities if the defendant is less than 4 years older than the victim." Just so we're clear, this means that the high school sexual experiences I described earlier which were illegal because we were on vacation in Massachusetts would have been just fine if we'd been at home.

In fact, some states focus on the age difference between the two individuals. The District of Columbia, for example, says that it's illegal to engage in sexual intercourse with someone who is under the age of 16 if the perpetrator is four or more years older than the victim. But other states like to make it even more complicated by taking into account the age of both parties. Washington state's laws say that sexual intercourse with someone who is at least 14 but less than 16 is illegal if the defendant is four or more years older but changes the age gap for victims under 14 "in cases where the victim is less than 14 years of age (three years), further decreasing if the victim is less than 12 years of age (two years)." This would mean that in both of these states the case of a 15-year-old girl with an 18-year-old boyfriend would not be illegal.

Other states, however, focus on the age of the perpetrator either on its own or along with the age of the victim. Both Nevada and Ohio, for example, say that perpetrators cannot be prosecuted if they are under 18, thus the two 16 year olds are safe from prosecution but the 15-year-old's 18 year-old boyfriend is not.

But wait, it gets even more complicated than that because many states make a distinction between sexual contact and sexual intercourse. That's right; there are instances in which activities that under different circumstances we might refer to as foreplay, sexplay, fooling around, or "outercourse" can be illegal depending on the age of the participants. In Connecticut, for example, engaging in *sexual intercourse* with someone who is less than 16 is legal under certain circumstances but *sexual contact* with someone who is less than 15 is illegal regardless of the age of the perpetrator.

Potential Nightmare Scenarios

So are we supposed to give our teens law books or maybe decoder rings as they head out on a weekend date? Don't we think teens already have enough to worry about when it comes to choosing which sexual behaviors they are going to engage in with a partner?

Obviously, one problem with creating an age of consent law is that there is no universal agreement as to when it is "okay" for teens to have sex. As Dr. Elizabeth Schroeder, the executive director of Answer, a national sexuality education organization that serves young people and the adults who teach them, explains:

> We always tell young people that there's no one right age at which it's okay to start being in a sexual relationship—because with a few exceptions, age is not necessarily the defining factor. We can all agree that, say, 11 or 12 is far too young to be in a sexual relationship, but as we get into the teen years, opinions vary. Readiness has to do with maturity, knowledge about and ability to practice safer sex, whether the decision is in line with that person's values, etc. I've known teens who are more responsible about their sexual relationships than some people in their 30s.

Clearly laws based solely on age do not see these distinction but it seems like those laws based on age differences aren't getting it either. We've all heard about cases like the ones discussed in the *Daily Beast* article and I'm sure we can all think of other nightmare scenarios; the mother who turns her daughter's slightly older boyfriend in because she doesn't like him, the young woman upset about being dumped who turns in her older boyfriend, or the guidance counselor who feels compelled to pass rumors on to authorities. Many of the sexual experts I spoke with also expressed concern for gay and lesbian young people whom they felt were even more vulnerable to irate parents who want to "throw the book" at an older partner who they blame for "turning their kid gay."

The expert were all distressed about the possibility of such cases and outrage over how these laws were being applied was a common refrain. J. Dennis Fortenberry, a professor of pediatrics at Indiana University who researches adolescent sexual behavior said: "This enthusiastic jailing under the guise of protection is in fact an abuse of power and sexual rights." Pepper Schwartz, an author and sociologist at the University of Washington, referred to these laws as "a very blunt dangerous instrument for a very complex culturally variable circumstance." She pointed out that such laws would cause any mother of a son to fear "that your child could do something unwise but not aggressive or without invitation that would ruin his life forever."

The Harmful Consequences of Prosecution

Many of the educators I spoke with pointed out just how normal and common sexual behavior among teens under the age of consent is. One study [by the Centers for Disease Control] found that 23 percent of 15-year-olds and 34 percent of 16-years-old have had vaginal intercourse. According to the CDC's Youth Risk Behavior Surveillance Survey, nearly two-thirds of high school student[s] have had sex before they graduate. Clearly we shouldn't be sending them all to jail instead of college. Fortenberry notes that given the average age of first sex is between 16 and 17, "the number of people you would have to prosecute if the law was uniformly and equally applied would [be] staggering."

And that is one of his main complaints with age of consent laws—they are not equally enforced or enforceable. Teens are in many ways at the mercy of an enraged parent or an over-eager law enforcement official. As one expert pointed out, "all you need is one police officer at lover's lane." Another expert I spoke with told me a story of case she had learned about many years ago involving a girl who was not quite 13 and a 17-year-old boy who had sex one time. The incident was brought to the attention of a guidance counselor who reported it to the authorities because she was under 14. Everyone involved in the case—both teens and both sets of parents—agreed that the sex was consensual and that if anything the girl was the aggressor in the incident. While they were able to prevent the teenage boy from going to prison, despite this agreement, they were not able to keep his name off the state's sex offender registry.

It is these registries that have experts most alarmed and upset because they have lifetime implications. States began to create such registries in the 1990s with the intention of protecting community members from violent sex offenders who were at a high risk of reoffending. The Reverend Debra Haffner, executive director of the Religious Institute, notes:

> These laws were never intended to place teenagers on offender registries for the rest of their lives. What we're seeing here is the confluence of two panics—that of teens having sex coupled with the panic about offenders.

She added that age of consent and registry laws, "Equate all kinds of legal violations so that this teenager is listed with people who are serial rapists of children."

Perpetuating Age-Old Stereotypes

I have argued many times that our society takes an inherently negative view of teen sexual behavior. Despite the fact that the majority of individuals do have sex at some point during their teenage years, adults continue to treat it as a problem that needs fixing rather than a normal part of growing up. And the application of these laws to teenage relationships seems like a natural—if not extreme—example of this.

These laws are based on the assumption that teens are incapable of giving consent and that adults need essentially to protect them from themselves. Fortenberry, for one, disagrees with that premise:

> My understanding of the evolving capacity of young people as they move through the period of time after puberty is that as a rule it involves the capacity to make distinctions that would allow them to accept or decline sex.

Most of the experts I spoke to also noted the inherent gender bias at the heart of these laws or at least the enforcement of them.

The laws perpetuate the age-old stereotypes of men as predators and women as helpless victims. As written modern laws are meant to be gender neutral, but Haffner points out that:

> The culture still says that boys with older girlfriends get lucky and girls with older boyfriends are exploited.

In doing so, says Schwartz:

> We negate the sexual agency of young women. We assume anything they do until a certain age has got to be victimization.

This is a dangerous precedent to set when what we ultimately want to ensure is that young women are able to see themselves as equal participants in sexual relationships—who have the same rights and the same responsibilities when it comes to sexual behavior.

It is also a very dangerous message to send to young men who are so often told that "boys will be boys" and even expected to be aggressive when it comes to sex. Schroeder argues that our culture "Wants boys who are predatory because that proves that they're real men," and that we teach them that "they can never say no to a sexual advance." It seems unfair then that there are laws that can punish young men for saying yes to what both parties believe is a consensual experience.

Age of Consent Laws Negatively Impact Young People's Sexual Health

We also have to remember that these laws have implications beyond the obvious ones for the young people involved. Reproductive health care providers, for example, fear the impact of these laws on their relationships with young people because in some states certain professionals, including educators and providers, must report any act or suspected act of statutory rape. What does this mean for the health care provider whose client tells them of a much older boyfriend?

Mandatory reporting laws are perhaps even more compli-cated than age of consent laws because this is often covered not in the statutory rape laws but in the child abuse laws and while some states declare statutory rape to be child abuse, others do not. The HHS [Department of Health and Human Services] re-port explains:

> In those states where the definition of child abuse does not explicitly refer to statutory rape, discrepancies between the le-gality of certain sexual activities and whether they are report-able offenses are more common.

For example, in Georgia all sexual activity with someone under 16 is illegal but such acts are only reportable offenses if the perpetrator is more than five years older than the victim. In some states the laws seem to contradict themselves. In Utah *sexual conduct* with someone who is between 16 and 18 is only illegal if the defendant is 10 or more years older than the victim. However, *sexual abuse* includes all acts of sexual intercourse, molestation, or sodomy with someone under 18 regardless of the age of the defendant and *sexual abuse* is a reportable offense.

Needless to say, health care providers are confused at best when it comes to their responsibilities and such confusion works its way into the exam room. What are health care providers sup-posed to do when a young woman reports being in a consensual relationship with an older male? Are they better off telling their client to keep the age of her partner to herself? The fear of course is that in either case young women will be deterred from seeking the reproductive health care they need.

It is also worth noting that certain far right groups have used the reporting of relationships between younger women and older men as a means to attack reproductive health providers, such as Planned Parenthood, that provide abortion. In 2002, for example, an anti-choice group hired an actress to call abortion clinics across the country pretending to be a 13-year-old girl who was pregnant by her 22-year-old boyfriend. The goal of cold calling campaign was to "catch" these organizations failing to report statutory rape. Other anti-choice organizations have used the cover of statutory rape laws to try and obtain health records of women who have gotten abortions.

Fostering Critical Thinking

Amid all the outrage over these laws, the experts with whom I spoke all understood that we do have an obligation to protect young people from exploitation. Haffner likened this to the need for sexual harassment laws in the workplace:

> We do have an interest in making it clear that there are laws to protect people when they don't have power.

Creating fair laws to do this, of course, remains a challenge.

One place to start, however, would be to change the classification of statutory rape laws in order to make a distinction between the teen lover whose partner was legally too young and the serial rapist or child molester. As Schwartz put it:

> These laws started out with a good intention—to stop seduction of children by adults—but the teenage years are a very different proposition. Even if we want to make it a crime for someone to have sex with a person more than three or four years younger or with a person under 13, sex offense isn't the crime. You're not a sex offender.

Or we might want to do away with our rush to punish teen sex and instead work to come to a better understanding—both as individuals and a society—of what consent really is. As educators, everyone I spoke to, wished for a national dialogue on these issues and for programs that would help teens handle consent issues. Fortenberry's wish list included giving teens:

> Good refusal skills as well as relationship literacy that helps them understand what a good relationship is and how to judge when they feel truly ready to have sex.

In my mind, pretty much all issues around teen sexual behavior come down to critical thinking. We want teens to be able look critically at a situation and assess whether it's a good idea to engage in any given sexual behavior. In *Talk About Sex*, a resource aimed directly at teens that we created while I was at SIECUS [Sexuality Information and Education Council of the United States], Monica Rodriguez [SIECUS president and CEO] and I asked teenagers to look at a number of factors when deciding what they wanted to do in a sexual relationship. We suggested they take into account the relationship (old friend, new acquaintance), the specific situation (upstairs at a party, in a parked car), and their motivations (to feel closer to a person, to gain popularity, to keep a partner from breaking up with them). We also suggested that they ask themselves if they had the other person's consent, if everyone was being honest, if they felt safe, if they felt exploited, and if they were protecting themselves and their partner from pregnancy and STDs.

I believe that given the skills to think critically about all of these aspects of sexual relationships many young people would themselves weed out the relationships that we as adults are most concerned about—whether it's a 15-year-old girl admitting that having sex with her 19-year-old boyfriend was really an attempt to prove she was mature enough to be with him or a 20-year-old boy questioning the wisdom of dating someone who is still in high school. But it is our responsibility as adults to teach them how to assess these situations.

It is also our responsibility as adults to think critically ourselves about the benefits and risks of the laws we make and how we apply them. No matter how good the intent behind it, there is something wrong with a law that forces a judge to brand a young man as a rapist thereby severely limiting his opportunities for housing and employment for the rest of his life simply for having sex with someone before her 16th birthday. And it is our responsibility as adults to fix it.

"*What many teens and pre-teens don't consider now is the long term implications of impulsive, foolish choices made today.*"

Sexting Is Immoral and Criminal

John L. Terry

In the following viewpoint, a danger awareness educator examines the negative consequences for teenagers involving sexting, the act of transmitting suggestive or lewd photos of oneself via cell phone. The author argues that this inappropriate behavior stems in part from a decline in moral restraint among young people and the ignorance or permissiveness of parents. He warns how those engaged in sexting fail to think about the consequences of their actions, which may include embarrassment, punishment, and even a criminal record. The author points out that several states have made sexting a felony, and he urges parents to teach their children about the legal and personal ramifications of this unwise act. John L. Terry is the regional director of the River Valley, Arkansas, National Security Alliance Women-Safe Network and Kid-Safe Network, two programs aimed at danger awareness education.

John L. Terry, "It's Called 'Sexting' and It's a Crime," EzineArticles.com, March 13, 2009. http://ezinearticles.com. Copyright © 2009 by Kid-Safe Communities. All rights reserved. Reproduced by permission.

The cell phone has revolutionized the way communications take place in today's culture. The world of Star Trek has reached beyond the big screen to become a modern day technological tool that has made wireless communication a common day occurrence for millions of people. No longer are consumers bound to hard-wired telephones of years past; the cellular phone has made it possible to communicate with just about anyone, anywhere. Advances in technology have taken cell phones from the size of a brick to the size of a credit card, and now incorporates a host of new features, including Internet-enabled cameras that capture images and record video that can be uploaded to the Web.

No longer just a tool for business, cell phones are now used to link individuals together, and are increasingly being used by teens and pre-teens to communicate with one another. Thousands of text messages travel wirelessly from phone to phone as a new generation of cell phone users chat endlessly back and forth. These next generation phones also share text, video and digital images quickly and efficiently.

The Legal Consequences of Sexting

But it's not just pictures of Fido and Calico that are being shared one with another. A recent study shows that 1 in 5 teen and pre-teen cell phone users are using their wireless phones to send inappropriate or nude pictures (or video) of themselves with other cell phone users. Often sent from girlfriend to boyfriend (following a trend set by two of the stars of High School Musical), these pictures are often shared with others without the sender's knowledge or consent. Whether forwarded to others to brag, or as a means of retaliation in the event of an argument, the end result is often humiliation, embarrassment, or degradation of the person featured in the shared image.

The practice is called "Sexting" and it's a crime. Yet few juveniles (and fewer parents) know this is the case. In some states, sexting is a misdemeanor, but in a growing number of others it is a felony. An increasing number of states view this as the transmission of child pornography (and prosecute it as such) if the images are of someone under the age of 18 (or if inappropriate images are sent to someone under age 18). And the courts are not just "slapping the wrist" of offenders any longer; as the proliferation of cases are filtering into the courts.

In a recent case in Florida, a 17-year old girl sent a nude picture of herself to her 18-year old boyfriend. After an argument, the 18-year old boy sent the nude picture to everyone in the girl's "friends" list, which unbeknownst to him included her teachers, parents, and close friends. The young man was arrested, charged and convicted of transmitting child pornography via an electronic medium and was ordered to register as a sex offender. He lost his job, was kicked out of college, and is unable to live with his Father because his dad lives too close to a school. He was also ordered to go through a sex offender's rehabilitation class, and will remain on the registered sex offender's list until the age of 45. His picture is featured on the state's website, and he has to daily deal with the humiliation and embarrassment for his actions.

The young girl who sent him the picture also faced embarrassment, ridicule and humiliation from friends and others who heard about the high profile case. The lives of two families were forever damaged because a young girl thought it "cool" to send naked pictures of herself to her boyfriend and subsequently having those images forwarded (without her knowledge or consent) to others by her boyfriend after a fight. Both actions were wrong, and both individuals (as well as their families) have had to deal with the consequences of wrong choices . . . and for the young boy, those consequences will follow him for the next 25–30 years.

Teen Sexting Occurs at an Alarming Rate

In Pennsylvania, three girls who sent nude or partially nude pictures of themselves to three boys in their school now face felony charges of distributing child pornography. A Texas eighth grader

Many people find "sexting"—the practice of sending sexually explicit texts or photos via cell phone—to be dangerous and detrimental to the future prospects of teenagers. © Dean Belcher/ Getty Images.

was jailed for sending a nude picture of himself to another student. In Virginia, two boys (ages 15 and 18) have been charged with solicitation and possession of child pornography with intent to distribute after law enforcement learned the teens sought nude pictures from three juveniles, one in elementary school. According to a report issued by the National Center for Missing and Exploited Children, of the 2100 children who were identified as victims of online porn, 1 in 4 initially sent the images to themselves. Some did it for fun, and others were tricked by adults they met online.

In another case in Pennsylvania, a 15-year old girl has been charged for sending nude pictures of herself over the Internet to a 27 year old she met online. The intent was not to jail her, but to help her get counseling and other help she needs, according to the District Attorney handling the case. He added the 27 year old has been sentenced to 10 years for having sex with the juvenile. In Ohio, 8 teens have been arrested for trading nude pictures of themselves with others. One of the girl's fathers found the images and reported authorities.

Yet every day this practice continues, and is proliferating at an alarming rate among today's youth.

Sexting Stems from a Lack of Moral Restraint

Cyberbullying is the use of any electronic medium to humiliate, ridicule, intimidate, embarrass, threaten or abuse another person. In a culture that uses sex to sell everything from underwear to toothpaste, today's teens and preteens often have no sense of morality when it comes to decency standards. In the 1960's, TV censors would not permit open-mouthed kisses to be shown, and even married couples slept in separate twin beds on many TV shows. A generation later, little (if anything) is left to the imagination . . . even in prime time. Music videos, movies, soap operas, and even (so-called) family television shows continue to push the decency boundaries to the point that few, if any, moral standards are enforced by the FCC [Federal Communications Commission]. Today's teens and pre-teens see so many sex acts on TV, they have accepted the lack of decency standards as normal.

Coupled with a growing lack of parental supervision and guidance, today's youth lack moral restraint and see no problem with sending inappropriate or nude pictures of themselves to others (or posting them online). What they don't understand is that once an image is posted on the Internet, it is forever there and can't be removed. Today's technology archives virtually all email, as well as postings to social networking (and other) websites. And images sent to another person's cell phone are now outside their control and can be posted to a website or shared with others without their knowledge or consent. Once forwarded to other cell phones by a third party, those images can be forwarded to countless others anywhere in the world.

But it's not just teens and pre-teens who are engaging in this activity. A small but growing number of adults, including married spouses, are sending inappropriate or nude pictures of themselves over cell phones. Those who should know better (and be setting a positive example for the younger generation to follow) are sadly illustrating a disturbing lack of conscience and moral fortitude by engaging in sexting.

Teens Fail to Understand the Long-term Consequences of Sexting

The saddest part of sexting is that the act of cyberbullying starts with the individual who actually sends a picture of himself (or herself) to another person. Sexting is humiliating to the person who sends his or her picture to another, whether they realize it or not . . . and this is compounded when those images are shared with others either by cell phone or posting online. The young girl who takes an inappropriate picture of herself and sends it to her boyfriend is just as guilty of cyberbullying as the boyfriend who shares it with others. Both acts are immoral, and could be considered a crime.

What many teens and pre-teens don't consider now is the long term implications of impulsive, foolish choices made today. Imagine the shock when a prospective employer conducts a background check on a recent high school or college graduate only to find inappropriate or nude pictures posted in a number of Internet archives. As previously stated, these images, once posted, are there forever and can be accessible to anyone who has Internet access. As these teens and pre-teens marry in the future, and their children begin to search online, how will these parents explain the fact their suggestive, inappropriate, or naked images are there?

A question that deserves to be asked is why do children need cell phones in the first place? While they do provide a measure of convenience (and security), the vast majority of children use cell phones solely for pleasure and not for other purposes. Parents spend hundreds (sometimes thousands) of dollars each year to provide cell phones almost exclusively so they can talk

A 2008 Poll Reveals Why Some Teens Engage in Sexting

Why do teens and young adults send or post sexually suggestive content?

- 51% of teen girls say pressure from a guy is a reason girls send sexy messages or images; only 18% of teen boys cited pressure from female counterparts as a reason.

- 23% of teen girls and 24% of teen boys say they were pressured by friends to send or post sexual content.

Among teens who have sent sexually suggestive content:

- 66% of teen girls and 60% of teen boys say they did so to be "fun or flirtatious"—their most common reason for sending sexy content.

- 52% of teen girls did so as a "sexy present" for their boyfriend.

- 44% of both teen girls and teen boys say they sent sexually suggestive messages or images in response to such content they received.

- 40% of teen girls said they sent sexually suggestive messages or images as "a joke."

- 34% of teen girls say they sent/posted sexually suggestive content to "feel sexy."

- 12% of teen girls felt "pressured" to send sexually suggestive messages or images.

National Campaign to Prevent Teen and Unplanned Pregnancy and CosmoGirl.com, Sex and Tech: Results from a Survey of Teens and Young Adults. *Washington, DC: National Campaign to Prevent Teen and Unplanned Pregnancy, 2008.*

to their friends, play games, or engage in web-based activities using their phones. And if the child is given a phone primarily for communication purposes with their family (or emergencies), do they really need a gadget-laden phone with all the bells and whistles (including Internet access or image capture capabilities)? Would not a basic cell phone suffice? How many instances are there where a landline is not readily available that a cell phone is a necessity, and not a luxury? If children are given a cell phone, are they mature enough to use it appropriately?

Plus there are no studies on the long-term health risks associated with cell phone use by children into adulthood.

What Parents Need to Know

It is important to note that if a parent is providing a cell phone to a child, and paying for the service, they should understand they could be held liable in any civil action taken by others as a result of an inappropriate use of the cell phone by their children. Some federal legislators are even considering a measure that would hold parents criminally liable if the child's phone is used for sexting or other inappropriate uses.

Parents should talk to their children about cell phone use (and etiquette). They should also regularly check their children's cell phones (and social networking sites, like Facebook, Orkut and MySpace) to make sure that there are no inappropriate images or content therein. As parents could be held liable for the content stored on or transmitted by their children's cell phones, they have a vested interest in actively monitoring that phone's usage. Children should understand the potential ramifications of posting inappropriate or nude pictures of themselves or others on cell phones or the Internet (including email), and that the consequences of these wrong choices can be devastating to themselves and others.

It's called "sexting," and it's a crime.

| "Enter the law—and the injuries of otherwise harmless teenage sexual shenanigans begin."

What's the Matter with Teen Sexting?

Judith Levine

In the following viewpoint, a civil libertarian explains that sexting—the transmission of lewd or suggestive images to and from minors—is simply an example of the sexual curiosity of young people. She believes it is unfair to criminalize this behavior under existing laws meant to deter child pornography. She maintains that those jurisdictions that continue to prosecute sexting cases as felonies are likely doing little to discourage the behavior but probably doing long-term harm to those charged. Judith Levine is a journalist and writer based in Vermont. She is the author of Harmful to Minors: The Perils of Protecting Children from Sex *and other books.*

Sex and predatory adults are not the biggest dangers teenagers face online. Their main risk is garden-variety kid-on-kid meanness.

Judith Levine, "What's the Matter with Teen Sexting?," *American Prospect*, January 30, 2009. Copyright © 2009 by the American Prospect. All rights reserved. Reproduced by permission.

A couple of weeks ago, in Greensburg, Pennsylvania, prosecutors charged six teenagers with creating, distributing, and possessing child pornography. The three girls, ages 14 and 15, took nude or seminude pictures of themselves and e-mailed them to friends, including three boys, ages 16 and 17, who are among the defendants. Police Captain George Seranko described the obscenity of the images: They "weren't just breasts," he declared. "They showed female anatomy!"

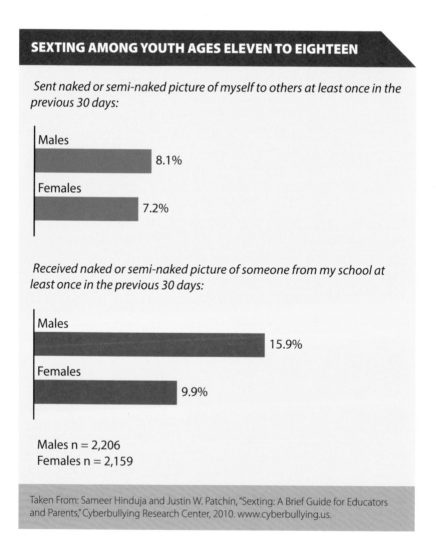

SEXTING AMONG YOUTH AGES ELEVEN TO EIGHTEEN

Sent naked or semi-naked picture of myself to others at least once in the previous 30 days:

Males
8.1%

Females
7.2%

Received naked or semi-naked picture of someone from my school at least once in the previous 30 days:

Males
15.9%

Females
9.9%

Males n = 2,206
Females n = 2,159

Taken From: Sameer Hinduja and Justin W. Patchin, "Sexting: A Brief Guide for Educators and Parents," Cyberbullying Research Center, 2010. www.cyberbullying.us.

Greensburg's crime-stoppers aren't the only ones looking out for the cybersafety of America's youth. In Alabama, Connecticut, Florida, New Jersey, New York, Michigan, Ohio, Pennsylvania, Texas, and Utah (at last count) minors have been arrested for "sexting," or sending or posting soft-core photo or video self-portraits. Of 1,280 teens and young adults surveyed recently by the National Campaign to Prevent Teen and Unplanned Pregnancy, one in five said they engaged in the practice—girls only slightly more than boys.

Seranko and other authorities argue that such pictures may find their way to the Internet and from there to pedophiles and other exploiters. "It's very dangerous," he opined.

How dangerous is it? Not very, suggests a major study released this month by Harvard's Berkman Center for Internet Studies. "Enhancing Child Safety and Online Technologies," the result of a yearlong investigation by a wide range of experts, concludes that "the risks minors face online are in most cases not significantly different from those they face offline, and as they get older, minors themselves contribute to some of the problems." Almost all youth who end up having sex with adults they meet online seek such assignations themselves, fully aware that the partner is older. Similarly, minors who encounter pornography online go looking for it; they tend to be older teenage boys.

But sex and predatory adults are not the biggest dangers kids face as they travel the Net. Garden-variety kid-on-kid meanness, enhanced by technology, is. "Bullying and harassment, most often by peers, are the most frequent threats that minors face, both online and offline," the report found.

Just as almost all physical and sexual abuse is perpetrated by someone a child knows intimately—the adult who eats dinner or goes to church with her—victims of cyber-bullying usually know their tormenters: other students who might sit beside them in homeroom or chemistry. Social-networking sites may be the places where kids are likely to hurt each other these days, but those sites, like the bullying, "reinforce pre-existing social relations," according to the report.

Similarly, young people who get in sexual or social trouble online tend to be those who are already at risk offline—doing poorly in school, neglected or abused at home, and/or economically impoverished. According to the Centers for Disease Control and Prevention, a child from a family whose annual income is less than $15,000 is 22 times more likely to suffer sexual abuse than a child whose parents earn more than $30,000.

Other new research implies that online sexual communication, no matter how much there is, isn't translating into corporeal sex, with either adults or peers. Contrary to popular media depiction of girls and boys going wilder and wilder, La Salle University sociologist and criminal-justice professor Kathleen A. Bogle has found that American teens are more conservative than their elders were at their age. Teen virginity is up and the number of sexual partners is down, she discovered. Only the rate of births to teenage girls has risen in the last few years—a result of declining contraceptive use. This may have something to do with abstinence-only education, which leaves kids reluctant or incompetent when it comes to birth control. Still, the rate of teen births compared to pregnancies always tracks the rate among adult women, and it's doing that now, too.

Like the kids finding adult sex partners in chat rooms, those who fail to protect themselves from pregnancy or sexually transmitted diseases and have their babies young tend to be otherwise at risk emotionally or socially. In other words, kids who are having a rough time in life are having a rough time in virtual life as well. Sexual or emotional harm *precedes* risky or harmful on- and offline behavior, rather than the other way around.

Enter the law—and the injuries of otherwise harmless teenage sexual shenanigans begin. The effects of the ever-stricter sex-crimes laws, which punish ever-younger offenders, are tragic for juveniles. A child pornography conviction—which could come from sending a racy photo of yourself or receiving said photo from a girlfriend or boyfriend—carries far heavier penalties than most hands-on sexual offenses. Even if a juvenile sees no lock-up time, he or she will be forced to register as a sex offender for 10 years or more. The federal Adam Walsh Child Protection Act of 2007 requires that sex offenders as young as 14 register.

As documented in such reports as Human Rights Watch's "No Easy Answers: Sex Offender Laws in the U.S." and "Registering Harm: How Sex Offense Registries Fail Youth and Communities" from the Justice Policy Institute, conviction and punishment for a sex crime (a term that includes nonviolent offenses such as consensual teen sex, flashing, and patronizing a prostitute) effectively squashes a minor's chances of getting a college scholarship, serving in the military, securing a good job, finding decent housing, and, in many cases, moving forward with hope or happiness.

Phillip Alpert says that sexting ruined his life. He had to register as a sex offender after e-mailing nude photos of his girlfriend taken when they were both minors. Some would argue that his punishment for sexting far outweighs his crime. © Ricardo Ramirez Buxeda/MCT/ Landov.

The sexual dangers to youth, online or off, may be less than we think. Yet adults routinely conflate friendly sex play with hurtful online behavior. "Teaching Teenagers About Harassment," [a] recent piece in the *New York Times*, swings between descriptions of consensual photo-swapping and incessant, aggressive texting and Facebook or MySpace rumor- and insult-mongering as if these were similarly motivated—and equally harmful. It quotes the San Francisco-based Family Violence Prevention Fund, which calls sending nude photos "whether it is done under pressure or not" an element of "digital dating violence."

Sober scientific data do nothing to calm such anxieties. Reams of comments flowed into the *New York Times* when it reported Dr. Bogle's findings. "The way TV and MUSIC is promoting sex and explicit content daily and almost on every network," read one typical post, from the aptly named MsKnowledge, "I would have to say this article is completely naive. The streets are talking and there [sic] saying teens and young adults are becoming far more involved in more adult and sexual activities than most ADULTS. Scientific data is a JOKE . . . pay attention to reality and the REAL world will tell you otherwise."

A better-educated interlocutor, NPR's "On the Media" host Brooke Gladstone, defaulted to the same assumption in an interview with one of the Harvard Internet task force members, Family Online Safety Institute CEO Stephen Balkam. What lessons could be drawn from the study's findings? Gladstone asked. "What can be and what should be done to protect kids?"

"There's no silver bullet that's going to solve this issue," Balkam replied. But "far more cooperation has got to happen between law enforcement, industry, the academic community, and we need to understand far better the psychological issues that are at play here."

It's unclear from this exchange what Gladstone believes kids need to be protected from or what issue Balkam is solving. But neither of them came to the logical conclusion of the Harvard study: that we should back off, moderate our fears, and stop thinking of youthful sexual expression as a criminal matter. Still, Balkam wants to call in the cops.

Maybe all that bullying is a mirror of the way adults treat young people minding their own sexual business. Maybe the "issue" is not sex but adults' response to it: the harm we do trying to protect teenagers from themselves.

Organizations to Contact

The editors have compiled the following list of organizations con-
cerned with the issues debated in this book. The descriptions are
derived from materials provided by the organizations. All have
publications or information available for interested readers. The
list was compiled on the date of publication of the present volume;
the information provided here may change. Be aware that many
organizations take several weeks or longer to respond to inquiries,
so allow as much time as possible.

Advocates for Youth
2000 M Street NW, Suite 750
Washington, DC 20036
(202) 419-3420 • fax: (202) 419-1448
website: www.advocatesforyouth.org

Advocates for Youth seeks to provide information for US youth
about reproductive and sexual health to encourage them to make
informed and responsible decisions. The organization focuses
on informing youth of their rights and advocating on behalf of
youth for these rights; respecting the ability of youth to make
choices about their sexual health; and ensuring that society takes
responsibility for providing young people with the tools and information they need to make good choices about their health.
The organization's website provides information about a range
of topics including abstinence, abortion, contraceptives, and
GLBTQ (gay, lesbian, bisexual, transgender, and queer) issues.

American Civil Liberties Union (ACLU)
125 Broad Street, 18th Floor
New York, NY 10004
(212) 549-2500

website: www.aclu.org

The ACLU works to protect the civil rights and liberties of all Americans, particularly historically underrepresented populations such as minorities, women, and youth. Freedom of speech, press, assembly, and religion, as well as the rights to equal protection, due process, and privacy are chief among the rights defended by the organization. The ACLU has been a longtime proponent of a woman's right to have an abortion, open access to contraception, and LGBT (lesbian, gay, bisexual, and transgender) rights for citizens of all ages. Detailed information about the campaigns spearheaded by the ACLU on these issues can be read on the organization's website.

American Life League (ALL)

PO Box 1350
Stafford, VA 22555
(540) 659-4171 • fax: (540) 659-2586
website: www.all.org

ALL is a grassroots, Catholic pro-life organization that believes in the sanctity of life from creation to natural death. Additionally, ALL opposes chemical birth control and sex education in public schools, believing parents should be the ones to teach their children about sex. The organization's website provides additional information to support ALL's stance on these issues. *Celebrate Life* is the organization's official publication.

Americans United for Life (AUL)

655 15th Street NW, Suite 410
Washington, DC 20005
(202) 289-1478
e-mail: info@aul.org
website: www.aul.org

AUL, founded in 1971, was the first national pro-life organization in the United States. The organization advocates for public

policy that outlaws abortion, legislates safety standards for abortion clinics, protects health-care professionals from being forced
to make reproductive health choices that violate their beliefs,
and ensures that parents have a say in their children's reproductive health decisions. Details about AUL's current campaigns can
be read on the organization's website.

Answer
Center for Applied Psychology, Rutgers University
41 Gordon Road, Suite C
Piscataway, NJ 08854
(732) 445-7929 • fax: (732) 445-5333
e-mail: answered@rci.rutgers.edu
website: http://answer.rutgers.edu

Answer is a national organization within the Rutgers University
psychology department that works to answer the questions teens
have about sex. Answer seeks to develop and train educators on
honest and balanced approaches to sex education. The organization's website, sexetc.org, provides teens with a one-stop desti-
nation for sex education information and state-by-state details
about sex education rights, age of minority and consent, abortion and contraception rights, and LGBTQ (lesbian, gay, bisexual, transgender, and queer) rights.

AVERT
4 Brighton Road
Horsham, West Sussex, RH13 5BA, UK
e-mail: info@avert.org
website: www.avert.org

AVERT is an international charity dedicated to preventing the
spread of HIV and AIDS. The group works with local organizations to develop community programs, provides information
to educate people around the world about HIV and AIDS, and
works with the public to respond to specific issues relating to

HIV/AIDS. The organization provides information on its website specifically for teens about sex and relationships and age of consent laws around the world.

Focus on the Family

Colorado Springs, CO 80995

(800) A-FAMILY, (800) 232-6459

e-mail: help@focusonthefamily.com

website: www.focusonthefamily.com

Focus on the Family is a Christian ministry that works on an international level to help families thrive according to Christian teachings. The organization opposes abortion in all circumstances, making an exception only if the mother could die by carrying the pregnancy to term. Focus on the Family also believes that individuals should only have sex if they are married, and schools should teach only abstinence-based sex education. Detailed position papers on these topics and others relating to teens' sex rights can be read on the Focus on the Family website.

Guttmacher Institute

125 Maiden Lane, 7th Floor

New York, NY 10038

(212) 248-1111, (800) 355-0244 • fax: (212) 248-1951

website: www.guttmacher.org

The Guttmacher Institute utilizes a combination of research, policy analysis, and public education to promote improved sexual and reproductive health rights for individuals around the world. The organization believes that women and families should have the right to choose the appropriate time for reproduction, and women should be able to have safe, legal abortions if they believe it is the correct choice for them. Information about abortion, adolescents, and contraceptives, in addition to other sex-related topics, can be accessed on the Guttmacher Institute website. The institute also publishes the periodicals *Guttmacher Policy Review,*

Perspectives on Sexual and Reproductive Health, and *International Perspectives on Sexual and Reproductive Health.*

Heritage Foundation

214 Massachusetts Ave. NE
Washington, DC 20002
(202) 546-4400
e-mail: info@heritage.org
website: www.heritage.org

The Heritage Foundation is a conservative public policy organization that develops and promotes policies created based on the ideals of free enterprise, limited government, individual freedom, traditional US values, and a strong national defense. The organization favors sex education that emphasizes the need for young people to abstain from sex when they are young, supports parental consent for minor abortion laws, and maintains that there should be limitations on teen access to certain types of contraceptives such as the "morning after" pill. Details of Heritage's stance on these topics and others relating to teen sex can be read on the organization's website.

National Abortion Federation (NAF)

1660 L Street NW, Suite 450
Washington, DC 20036
(202) 667-5881 • fax: (202) 667-5890
e-mail: naf@prochoice.org
website: www.prochoice.org

NAF is a national organization representing abortion providers in North America. The members of the organization share the belief that all women should be allowed to decide what medical decisions are appropriate for their lives with the assistance of their medical care providers. NAF thus works to support a health-care system that provides safe, legal, and accessible abortion care for all women. Annual reports published by the organization on the state of abortion care as well as detailed information on topics such as parental consent laws and minors' ability to have abortions can be found on the NAF website.

National Right to Life Committee (NRLC)

512 10th Street NW
Washington, DC 20004
(202) 626-8800
e-mail: NRLC@nrlc.org
website: www.nrlc.org

NRLC is a national organization of individuals that supports pro-life initiatives and opposes abortion. The committee's website provides information about abortion, the dangers of abortion, and reasons why other alternatives are preferable to abortion. Fact sheets provide access to information about pro-life topics, and visitors to the website can find details about current legislation and legislative action being taken by the NRLC.

Planned Parenthood

434 W. 33rd Street
New York, NY 10001
(212) 541-7800 • fax: (212) 245-1845
website: www.plannedparenthood.org

Planned Parenthood is a national organization that provides affordable sexual and reproductive health care for both men and women and advocates to advance women's health and safety, reduce the number of unintended pregnancies, and safeguard the right of both individuals and families to make their own appropriate reproductive choices. In the Info for Teens section of the organization's website, visitors can find articles on a wide range of topics such as parental consent, access to contraceptives, and sex and sexuality.

For Further Reading

Books

Carolyn E. Cocca, *Jailbait: The Politics of Statutory Rape Laws in the United States.* Albany: State University of New York Press, 2004.

Heather Corinna, *S.E.X.: The All-You-Need-to-Know Progressive Sexuality Guide to Get You Through High School and College.* New York: Marlowe and Company, 2007.

J. Shoshanna Ehrlich, *Who Decides?: The Abortion Rights of Teens.* Santa Barbara, CA: Praeger, 2006.

N.E.H. Hull, Williamjames Hoffer, and Peter Charles Hoffer, eds., *The Abortion Rights Controversy in America: A Legal Reader.* Chapel Hill: University of North Carolina Press, 2004.

Tom Jacobs, *Teens Take It to Court: Young People Who Challenged the Law—and Changed Your Life.* Minneapolis: Free Spirit, 2006.

Holly Kreider et al., *188 Scientific Facts About Teen Sex, Contraception, Pregnancy, Parenting, and Sexually Transmitted Infections.* Los Altos, CA: Sociometrics, 2009.

Judith Levine, *Harmful to Minors: The Perils of Protecting Children from Sex.* Cambridge, MA: Da Capo, 2003.

Kristin Luker, *When Sex Goes to School: Warring Views on Sex—and Sex Education—Since the Sixties.* New York: Norton, 2006.

Ian Shapiro, ed., *Abortion: The Supreme Court Decisions, 1965–2007.* Indianapolis: Hackett, 2008.

Sabrina Weill, *The Real Truth About Teens and Sex: From Hooking Up to Friends with Benefits—What Teens Are*

Thinking, Doing, and Talking About, and How to Help Them Make Smart Choices. New York: Perigee, 2005.

Periodicals and Internet Sources

Associated Press, "Study: Parent Notification Law Cuts Abortions," April 8, 2006. www.msnbc.msn.com.

Janine Benedet, "The Age of Innocence: A Cautious Defense of Raising the Age of Consent in Canadian Sexual Assault Law," *New Criminal Law Review*, Fall 2010.

Russell L. Christopher and Kathryn H. Christopher, "The Paradox of Statutory Rape," *Indiana Law Journal*, Spring 2012.

Mikaela Conley, "Poor Teens Lack Access to Emergency Contraception," ABC News, January 24, 2012. http://abc news.go.com.

Laura Davis and Emily Bridges, "School Based Health Centers Should Provide Contraception to Teens," *Journal of Applied Research on Children*, 2011.

eSchool News, "Teen 'Sexting': Less Common than Parents, Educators Might Fear," December 6, 2011. www.eschool news.com.

Sandy M. Fernandez, "A Young Girl's Sexting Trauma: 'I Was Naked, Out in the World,'" *Redbook*, November 2011.

Scott Lemieux, "Bypassing Young Women's Abortion Rights," *American Prospect*, August 17, 2007. http://prospect.org.

Dalia Lithwick, "Teens, Nude Photos and the Law," *Newsweek*, February 23, 2009.

Kathryn Jean Lopez, "Parental Consent for Abortion Is Simply Common Sense," *Seattle Times*, June 3, 2005. http://commu nity.seattletimes.nwsource.com.

J. Bryan Lowder, "16 Going on 17: Age-of-Consent Laws, Explained," *Slate*, February 22, 2011. www.slate.com.

Maya Manian, "Functional Parenting and Dysfunctional Abortion Policy: Reforming Parental Involvement Legislation," *Family Court Review*, April 2012.

Julia Halloran McLaughlin, "Crime and Punishment: Teen Sexting in Context," *Perm State Law Review*, 2010.

Michael H. Meidinger, "Peeking Under the Covers: Taking a Closer Look at Prosecutorial Decision-Making Involving Queer Youth and Statutory Rape," *Boston College Journal of Law and Social Justice*, Spring 2012.

Todd Melby, "When Teens Get Arrested for Voluntary Sex," *Contemporary Sexuality*, February 2006.

Torsten Ove and Marylynne Pitz, "Teen Rights to Abortion in Dispute," *Pittsburgh Post-Gazette*, March 29, 2012. www.post-gazette.com.

Index